RESILIENCE

*How to Bounce
Back When the Going
Gets Tough!*

RESILIENCE

*How to Bounce Back
When the Going
Gets Tough!*

FREDERIC FLACH, M.D.

A SELF-HELP CLASSIC™
HATHERLEIGH PRESS
New York

A SELF-HELP CLASSIC™
published by Hatherleigh Press

Copyright © 1997 by Frederic F. Flach, M.D.

Hatherleigh Press
1114 First Avenue, Suite 500
New York, NY 10021
1-800-906-1234

The patients represented in this book are composites of many people and ideas.
They do not represent specific individuals, either living or dead.

The ideas and suggestions contained in this book are not intended as a substitute
for consulting with a physician. All matters regarding your health require medical
supervision.

Library of Congress Cataloging-in-Publication Data

Flach, Frederic F.
    Resilience: how to bounce back when the going gets tough! / Frederic
Flach.
        p.   cm.
    Published in 1988 with subtitle: Discovering a new strength at times of
stress.
    Includes bibliographical references and index.
    ISBN 1-886330-95-6 (alk. paper)
    1. Stress (Psychology)   2. Resilience (Personality trait)   3. Mental
health.   I. Title.
    RC455.4.S87F555   1997
    155.9'042—dc21   97-7161
                                                                                            CIP

Designed by Dede Cummings Designs
Printed in Canada on acid-free paper ♾
10 9 8 7 6 5 4 3 2 1

To the late Gerard Murphy, S. J.,
who, when asked to recommend
me for medical school, told me he
felt my gifts went beyond those
required of a physician, but, if I persisted
in my wish to become a doctor,
I should surely become a psychiatrist.

CONTENTS

ACKNOWLEDGMENTS

F EW DISCOVERIES take place entirely in a vacuum. While many people might like to take full credit for their new visions, the fact is we are always indebted to the past, to those thinkers who have set the stage for whatever it may be that we have come upon.

In developing my concept of disruption and reintegration as a necessary part of the human being's adaptation to change, and resilience in particular as the strength we all require to cope with this recurring cycle successfully, I am indebted to the work of many predecessors. Among them are physiologist Walter Cannon, who first defined biological homeostasis, and Karl Menninger who, in his classic book *The Vital Balance,* applied the model of homeostasis to the organization of our personalities; Hans Selye, with whom I enjoyed a number of personal dialogues, for his concept of stress; psychiatrist Ivor Browne, and indirectly his source, Nobel Prize–winning physicist Ilya Prigogine, for the term "bifurcation point." My communications with Arthur Koestler, Sir George Pickering, Sidney Parnes, Anthony Storr, and many others enriched my ideas about the nature of the creative process and its relevance not only to mankind's evolution but to the quality of our everyday lives as well.

Putting the concept of resilience into words, emphasizing its importance while making it truly accessible to the reader, has been a singular challenge. To this end I am indebted to Nancy van Itallie, Joëlle Delbourgo, and Wilhemina Austin for their insightful, invaluable editorial help.

I must also express my gratitude to so many people, patients, mentors, friends, and acquaintances who have through our relationships given me the opportunity to observe resilience at work firsthand. Their stories run throughout the pages of this book, carefully concealed as composites, of course, so that while none of the cases represent or define any particular individual they nonetheless resemble bits and pieces of all our lives.

−Frederic Flach, M.D.

INTRODUCTION

T HE CONCEPT OF RESILIENCE has probably been brewing within my subconscious mind for a very long time. Undoubtedly it was stimulated by the study of classics in college, but it only took form after I had become a physician and psychiatrist and after I had come to know the meaning of stress, adversity, disruption, and renewal within the lives of my patients and friends, and in my own life as well.

In some ways resilience is an idea whose truth will seem obvious once we give it due consideration. Yet, it is quite complex, relevant not only to each of us as individuals, but also to the survival and health of our families and institutions and of society itself.

What is resilience? It's the term I've chosen to describe the psychological and biological strengths required to successfully master change. Over the past thirty years, I've had the opportunity to observe how patients in therapy recover and become more integrated and effective than they were before. I have considered how people subject to major catastrophes and terrible hardships survived. I have noted the abilities that a wide variety of men and women I have known have called upon to cope with important, potentially dangerous turning points in their lives. Such data has permitted me to assemble a profile of resilience, one that we can all find extremely useful, in fact essential, if we are to stay in command of our lives.

There are certain resilient personality traits: Creativity. The ability to tolerate pain. Insight into ourselves and what we are going through at any particular phase in our lives. Independence of spirit. Self-respect. The ability to restore self-esteem when it is diminished or temporarily lost. A capacity for learning. The ability to make and keep friends. Freedom to depend on others, with the skill to set proper limits on the depth of our dependency. A perspective on life that offers a vital, evolving philosophy within which we can interpret all that we experience and from which we can discover some measure of personal meaning.

Of course, resilience is not a purely psychological issue. It's physical too. Being resilient demands that our bodies' physiological processes, activated by stress, function effectively.

Moreover, the world around us also has a profound influence on how well we can cultivate and exercise resilience. An example of this is the presence or absence of a network of human beings who constitute a meaningful system of support. There may or may not be a genuine give and take in relationships so that, when we need them, people who care for us are there, and, when they need us, we are there for them. Our family structures, our working conditions, our entire culture, possess characteristics which can thwart our resilience or enhance it.

Over the years, I have had the opportunity to study organizations as well as individuals. While institutional structures are not the main focus of this book, they are, after all, human creations. They are themselves subject to stress and change, and must acquire and preserve resilience no less than we do as individuals.

I first expressed this concept of resilience in 1966 in an article I wrote about the influence of the philosopher Teilhard de Chardin on my thinking as to the nature of psychiatric illness and the role psychotherapy plays in enabling patients to recover. Chardin, in his remarkable book *The Phenomenon of Man*, envisioned the contemporary world as caught up in a major shift in evolution, one primarily characterized by psychological and social changes rather than purely physical ones. By analogy, I suddenly saw many of my patients caught up in a similar, but highly personal, evolutionary change. Their personalities were shattered (and often the structures of their lives as well) and they were in a state of chaos, preparing themselves for a new and higher level of adaptation.

By 1974, when I wrote *The Secret Strength of Depression,* I had come to see falling apart, at least as far as depression was concerned, not so much as an unfortunate event, but often as a necessary prelude to personal renewal following significantly stressful events. In the years since, I have broadened my thinking beyond depression to define a cycle of falling apart and subsequently putting the pieces of ourselves and our lives together again in a new form, as a central and recurring theme throughout the human life cycle.

The concept of resilience has also enabled me to formulate a very different way to view mental health and illness. I began to look at many of my patients as being among the healthiest people I knew. Many of them had appropriately collapsed in the face of significant stress and change. What on the surface may have looked like a failure to cope was, in fact, evidence of resilience. The temporary state of confusion and emotional anguish in which they found themselves represented a singular opportunity to resolve old wounds, discover new ways to deal with life, and effectively reorganize themselves. Most importantly, they recognized the nature of the state in which they found themselves and knew enough to seek professional help.

In contrast, I began to look at many other people, some of whom prided themselves on never falling apart, as essentially unwell. They seemed much less able to learn from experience. They lacked insight. They generated innumerable problems for those around them, and they were far more vulnerable in the long run to the impact of change.

Of course, falling apart only represents the initial phase in the cycle of responding resiliently to stress. Resilience also means the strength to contain within reasonable limits the extent of personal disruption, and to reassemble the pieces of ourselves and our lives afterwards. When we cannot, then we risk being ill in another and more obvious way, by being trapped in a persistent, chronic state of dysfunction.

To some, the idea that everything human can fall apart episodically, especially under seriously stressful conditions, and must be renewed in order to survive and grow, may not seem novel. However, that we are *mandated* to do so by nature represents a very different emphasis indeed.

Consider the life cycle. It is marked by turning points, when change is the order of the day. Some are predictable, such as entering adolescence, graduating from school, getting married, becoming a parent, reaching middle age, retiring. Others, such as business or personal reversals, are not; they most likely will appear in everyone's life, although just when they will and what form they may take usually cannot be foreseen. Each period of change is necessarily stressful, for it involves conflict between a powerful force that operates to keep things exactly as they've been, and another powerful force that commands us to move forward and embrace new conditions. Stressful times are, by their very nature, disruptive. They rarely take place without some degree of pain, and are accompanied by a risk that we may not pass through them successfully. How much chaos will accompany any particular period of change will be determined to some degree by the intensity and extent of the changes taking place. Then, too, one particular turning point may produce more upheaval in one person's life than in another's. You may encounter the most intense turbulence of your life as an adolescent, while I may meet mine in middle age, and someone else may run into his or hers quite unexpectedly somewhere in between.

One might well ask: Has this not always been true? Have we not always been subject to stress and the need to master change? Of course. Resilience lies at the heart of human evolution. History is filled with the biographies of men and women whose greatness was achieved primarily through the resilience with which they met and overcame adversities.

But now we must face the fact that we all live in radically different times. It is one thing to go through periods of personal disruption and recover when the world around us is relatively stable. It is quite another to have to do so when the rate at which change is taking place throughout the world has become incredibly accelerated and whole cultures find themselves on the verge of disarray. More and more, each of us is at greater risk. We have little choice but to take the responsibility for weathering change very much unto ourselves.

The most encouraging observation I've made over all these years is that resilience is a strength most of us can develop with thought and practice.

PART I

Stress and the Law of Disruption and Reintegration: Conditions that Demand Resilience

1

The Far Side of Stress

ARE THINGS really moving at a faster pace today, or do we just imagine it? Do we all, in fact, live with more stress than people did a generation ago? Are we at greater risk that stress will cause us to become mentally or physically disabled, or to die suddenly, running to return a net ball on a tennis court on a beautiful spring afternoon?

Just what is stress anyway? Is it, as many of us envision, a culprit, something that evokes tension, makes us anxious or irritable, raises our blood pressure or causes our stomach to hurt, ruins our marriage and our career? Or is there another side to stress, some constructive purpose that it serves in the interests of our survival and growth?

Our current ideas about stress are of quite recent origins. Only a few decades ago, Professor Hans Selye first defined and described it as a variety of forces that induce protective physiological changes when we are under attack. The original formulation of stress was obtained by observing the response of living organisms to alien agents. Ours to bacteria, for example: Infection attacks the body. The immune systems are engaged to repel the invaders. Nonspecific reactions occur, such as fever and a rapid heart rate. White blood cells proliferate. When and if we win the battle, the systems that have been activated to defend our bodies settle down. Our temperature returns to normal. So does our pulse. We no longer feel "sick," although it may take us a little while to feel like our old selves again.

And one more change may take place. Our successful venture in self-defense may leave us with greater strength to deal with similar infections in the future. In fact, as in the case of such viral diseases as chicken pox, measles, and mumps, our bodies will have produced antibodies, and we may remain immune to future attacks by the same organism.

The physiological concept of stress was quickly extended to take into consideration triggers that were neither noxious organisms nor toxic substances. Psychological and social stresses were added to the list of challenges that require us to muster our defenses to overcome threats to our survival. An insult to my self-esteem or the loss of someone I love can produce significant physical as well as emotional responses. Through a complex system of communication that connects our senses with our brains and our brains with every location throughout our bodies, disturbing events are registered and reacted to physically as well as psychologically. Something psychobiological happens every time we are jolted by fear or agitated by anger, or even when we experience such positive feelings as the exhilaration of joy, convulsive laughter, or passionate love.

When the moment has passed and the period of stress is over—or as we may be forced to adjust to the reality that the stressful situations are not about to go away and may extend over a prolonged time period—the physiological stress responses must subside and return to a state of normal equilibrium again, resting, ready for some new, often unpredictable assault that may appear in the future. However, these physical stress responses differ greatly from what we may expect to go through psychologically. Except in the case of immunization (when the state of disruption passes and a new synthesis occurs), our bodies will return to their pre-existing state of homeostasis, or balance. In stark contrast, the psychological changes that accompany stress reactions should lead to a new, more complex and adaptive structure that is qualitatively different from that which preceded it. In other words, we should have learned something from what we have been through. We should emerge better put together and more qualified to deal with life's challenges because of our experience.

I recently had lunch with a friend of some years, a forty-six-year-old senior executive in a medium-sized computer software company, who could accurately be described as falling apart in the face of stress. He confided to me that his doctors had fruitlessly spent weeks employing the most modern diagnostic techniques to determine the source of his year-old, persistent complaints of leg pains, shortness of breath, and inability to concentrate on his work. He was obsessed with the thought that he might be suffering with some fatal illness, and was increasingly discouraged by the doctors' inability to discover a physical basis for his dysfunction.

I knew him to be a highly intelligent, hard-driving, successful person, well educated, more or less happily married, financially secure. However, I also knew he was quite rigid, with excessively high expectations for himself and his life, and I believed he probably lacked the insight and flexibility he would need to effectively weather the sudden and profound changes taking place in both his personal and his professional lives. At home, his eldest child, a twenty-year-old son, had been discovered using cocaine; his youngest child, a daughter, had just left to begin college. At work, for the third time in a decade, technological advances by competitors threatened to make his most recent and most important product line obsolete, and several of his key employees had departed for jobs elsewhere that paid better.

"Everything seems out of control," he said. "At business school, they believed they were teaching us how to manage change. They even encouraged us to initiate it. But things seem to be happening so fast and so unexpectedly nowadays, I don't feel able to control anything in my life. I feel like a failure as a businessman, as a parent.

"My doctors have told me my symptoms are all due to

pressure. I find that hard to believe," my friend said. "Sure, I have problems. So does everyone. But we're supposed to ride them out. I thought we were better prepared to deal with stress than our parents were. We certainly hear enough about it. My father certainly knew what stress was, firsthand. He grew up in the Depression years. He commanded a platoon in France in the Second World War. He survived."

I hastened to point out that I did indeed believe we experience more stress than our parents did, living, as we do, in a period of rapid and dramatic change. Most of the technological advances that have been made in the entire history of mankind have taken place in this century. These have radically altered the ways in which we move about on the earth and in space, how we communicate across vast distances, whether we cluster in communities or isolate ourselves in large urban areas. The jet airplane and the television set have profoundly reduced the size of the earth as we perceive and experience it. The nightly news is watched in remote islands in the Caribbean half an hour after it's been seen in New York or Chicago, and the airports of the world have brought cultures and peoples into immediate contact with each other, a confrontation that once appeared only in photos in the pages of *National Geographic*. The homes we live in, our economies, our social structures, and the work we perform are beginning to assume unfamiliar shapes. Even the information we have about ourselves—obtained from a vast array of social and scientific disciplines that can trace our history by means of radioisotopes and visualize in color the workings of our brains— has mushroomed to such an extent that how we view ourselves as human beings has been seriously challenged. All this will continue to take place at an ever-increasing rate, often seeming to be, as my friend described his own predicament, out of control.

Nor are we better able to cope with such stress, although we can learn to be. Until recently, we could rely much more on external structures to guide and protect us in our journey through life. Family life was more intact. Uniform values were widely shared. The chances were that we would live in the same community among familiar friends for most of our years. If we trained ourselves in some particular skill, we'd be likely to pursue that occupation for most of our working lives. The structures of society—its churches, governments, institutions, and expectations—promised a measure of permanence and predictability.

These bulwarks are no longer in place. More and more in free societies, the challenge of organizing ourselves and our worlds, and of reorganizing these after periods of disruption, rests largely on our own shoulders.

Tug-of-War

To grasp the meaning of stress more fully, we must understand the power all living structures possess to maintain themselves in states of relative coherence. This power is called homeostasis. The word is derived from Latin; *homeo* means "same," and *stasis* means "lack of motion." It is a biological force that acts to preserve the status quo, and to restore it after it has been disturbed.

The nineteenth-century French physiologist Claude Bernard was the first to describe the idea that each person's body represents a stabilized, internal milieu. It has vital mechanisms necessary to sustain its own autonomy, separate from its environment. In order to survive, we must keep such basic elements as temperature, blood pressure, pulse rate, respiratory rate, and acid-base balance within certain ranges. Failing to do so, we cease to exist.

Furthermore, this constancy must be sustained in the face of such changing external conditions as cold, heat, the need for sudden exertion, and those times when food intake is severely limited. For example, physical exertion accelerates the heart rate; with rest, and in the absence of disease, this rate returns to a normal level. This phenomenon is the basis of the cardiac stress test that many physicians use to ascertain how sound our hearts and vascular systems are.

This self-preserving adaptive capacity is present in all healthy people, although it is less developed in the very young and weaker in the very old. The infant has not yet developed the ability to exert such control; for example, if you raise the temperature of his environment, his body temperature tends to follow suit. In the elderly, this capacity is diminished; they are, for example, much more sensitive to cold weather, and their blood vessels lose the elasticity characteristic of youth.

The model of homeostasis can be applied as well to the organization of our personalities. Successful coping—meeting life's challenges, overcoming adversities, and, particularly, moving from one phase in the natural life cycle to the next—involves our ability to sustain our psychological coherence in the face of stress or if we have lost such coherence, as is often the case, to regain it afterward, although usually in a somewhat altered form. The traditional point of view—one to which I take strong exception—has held that a loss of personality homeostasis as a result of provocative events is the beginning point of illness; the more severe the disruption, the more serious the malady. Implicit in such a theory is the assumption that come what may, personality homeostasis will ordinarily be well maintained. Even those who have progressed in their thinking from such an inflexible vision to the point of allowing for some degree of breakdown under stress nonetheless believe that recovery consists essentially of the restoration of the preexisting homeostatic structure as it had always been. Even they would not regard falling apart as a desirable or necessary experience.

The closest that behavioral scientists have come to envisioning the human being as subject to continual movement and change is embodied in what is called systems theory. Here, the idea that we are organized, autonomous creatures, static, and once and for all defined, who defend our personalities against the ravages of external change, has been modified, giving way to the concept that we are part of open systems, in constant contact with, influencing, and being influenced by, our environments. Our minds and bodies constitute structures that are themselves continually undergoing various degrees of change. In turn, we are interacting with all other living structures that exist in the world around us—family, social networks, business or governmental enterprises, communities, nations, the biosystem, the universe. These structures themselves are also governed by a similar need to maintain homeostasis, but, at the same time, are subject to ongoing pressure of change.

The trouble with theory, however, is that it often makes remote, academic, even unreal the intense, meaningful struggles that take place in the battleground of life. The pressure that change can place on the forces of homeostasis can be very intense, painful, disturbing, overwhelming. A conflict is necessarily set up, a tug-of-war, between the mandate for a new homeostasis and the counterpressure exerted by the forces that act to preserve things as they have been.

Resistance to change is a universal phenomenon, and when pitted against change, it gives rise to a fear that ultimately intensifies the conflict. All too commonly, however, most of us are gifted at blocking out of consciousness things that threaten us, paying little or no attention to them until we become so distraught that we have no other choice but to heed what is taking place. Nowhere is such resistance so profound as when meaningful change speaks to the issue of who and what we are, as well as to the definition of the structure of the world in which we live. For such landmarks are as important to our everyday identification and functioning as our personal names. Once we have grown accustomed to a certain view of ourselves and those around us, we can be terrified by and fight vigorously against anything new or different. However, existing homeostases must break down—sooner, one hopes, rather than later—to set the stage for what is to come.

2

The Law of Disruption and Reintegration

FROM MY earliest days as a medical student, until I had been practicing psychiatry for nearly ten years, I thought that people could be divided into two major categories: the sick and the well. Those who suffered with depression and other forms of emotional distress or who were unable to carry out the daily responsibilities of their lives, and who had sought refuge in consulting rooms and hospitals staffed by doctors in long, white coats were sick. The rest of the world, I presumed, was well.

I vividly recall the defeated look on the faces of so many patients whom I worked with in those days, people in crisis. Martin Wall was a fifty-four-year-old man who walked into my office slowly, awkwardly, looking around the room trying to decide where he should sit. His gray, pinstriped suit was consistent with the popular image of his occupation, banker. But as he slumped in the black captain's chair and struggled to speak, he reminded me of a soldier who had just been brought back from the front lines suffering battle fatigue.

I pieced together his history. Martin Wall's only son had been severely injured in a riding accident a year earlier. Thrown from his horse, he suffered a serious fracture of his spine and would never walk again. Since then, the relationship between Martin and his wife had become strained, as each quietly held the other somehow responsible for the tragedy. He had gone on working, trying to keep his composure, as long as he was able; now, it seemed, he could not go on any longer. His wife had begun to drink. Whatever closeness they had known in the past had been destroyed. Even though they had three other children, all girls, they found no consolation in their family life, which had been torn apart no less than Martin's own self.

I presumed Martin Wall was sick and treated him accordingly, with psychotherapy and antidepressant drugs. My goal was to restore him to the health he had once enjoyed. I recognized the role that terrible stress had played in triggering his illness, but nonetheless assumed that there must be something wrong with him. Otherwise, wouldn't he have been able to handle things better, even something as awful as his son's disability? For a family that had apparently been functioning well, didn't there have to be something unhealthy for it to be so devastated? I expected grief, but I could understand neither why it had lasted so long nor why things had gotten so out of control.

Martin Wall did recover. He was able to resume his work; his family life regained a semblance of order, on the surface at least. But my contact with him and with many other people like him who were experiencing the effects of stressful life experiences made me begin to wonder. What should we really expect of ourselves when significant stress occurs in our lives? I know what we would like to be able to do—cope with change with equanimity. We would all prefer to ride out the turbulence painlessly. But what if that ideal of successfully coping is simply not possible? What if, in fact, it is actually counterproductive to our health and personal maturity?

When I was thirty-nine years old, I experienced a life crisis of my own, which served to crystallize my answers to these questions. Within a few months, my father died, my mother, her memory gone, was placed in a nursing home, my eldest child fell seriously ill, and I found myself unexpectedly facing divorce. Although I fought to maintain my equilibrium, I realized I was falling apart. It grew increasingly difficult to read, to listen to patients, to lecture medical students. I would lie in bed at night, tense, restless, finally falling asleep after a couple of hours only to wake up before dawn exhausted, dreading the day to come. Part of my mind kept telling me that what I was going through was normal grief. Another part, conditioned by years of professional training, applied medical terminology to my distress, a labeling that served only to intensify it. I fully believed that I should have been able to weather this crisis with greater fortitude, and certainly without compromising my ability to work. It was, to say the least, humiliating.

I stopped work for several months and tried to sort things out. I diverted myself in a number of ways—by traveling, for instance. Slowly, painfully, I began to put the pieces of my life together. My father was gone; now, I was the father. Over the years, I had grown quite dependent on the structure of my life; now, much of it had vanished, and I was faced with the need to create a new structure for myself and my family. For the first time in my life, I really understood what many of my patients must have felt—helplessness, the feeling of being defeated, a desperate search for hope, the day-by-day effort to reorganize their lives. And for the first time, I fully grasped how unimaginative and shortsighted I had been in my evaluation of people like Martin Wall.

I came to realize that significantly stressful events, by their very nature, *must* shake us up and often disrupt the structures of the world around us as well. Moreover, such turbulence has to be accompanied by distress, which can range from mild unhappiness, anxiety, or impatience all the way to a state of profound anguish in which we might seriously question who and what we are and the nature of the personal worlds we inhabit.

This insight gave me a totally different way to view stress. I began to see falling apart as a normal—in fact, necessary—response to significant changes within ourselves or in our environments; this would hold true even if such episodes became dramatic enough to permit doctors to make traditional medical or psychiatric diagnoses. By the same token, we would be faced with the challenge of being able to reorganize ourselves and our lives afterward. In fact, this process might well be nature's mandate, forcing us to forfeit obsolete perceptions and ways of viewing things in favor of new, more complex homeostases more suited to our present and future survival.

The points in life when such major shifts occur can be called *bifurcation points*—a term derived from the language of contemporary physics representing moments of extreme change. This is when we become severely destabilized. Our internal or external structures may disintegrate into chaos, and the eventual outcome of such chaos is totally unpredictable. For at such times, we are at great risk. We may remain forever more or less destabilized. We may even form a new homeostasis structured around

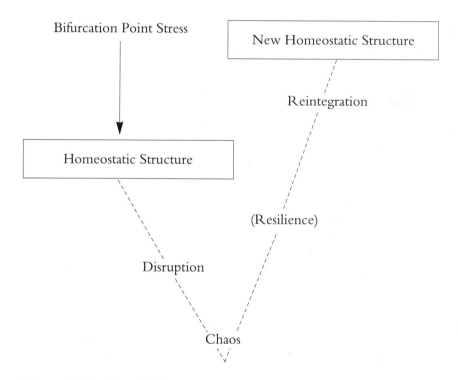

Figure 1. *The Normal Disruption-Reintegration Cycle*

disability, anguish, and inadequate coping behavior. Or, under optimal circumstances, the stage may be set for reintegration into a new and more effective level of personal coherence. The preceeding diagram illustrates the normal cycle of disruption and reintegration.

At first I saw such disruptions as events confined to major bifurcation points in life, occurring primarily when we have been subjected to severe stresses, large-scale, noisy affairs that are loud and clear, most often happening when our internal homeostasis has been shattered and the structure of our external world has exploded simultaneously, when our future, unpredictable in any event, is at serious risk. This is what Martin Wall experienced during his episode of depression. It is what I myself went through following my father's death. Then I saw that bifurcation points do not occur only when serious and significantly traumatic events have taken place, more or less unexpectedly, but that they recur regularly throughout our normal life cycle as we pass from one phase in life to the next.

Gradually, I also began to see that the law of disruption and reintegration itself does not apply only to our experiences during major bifurcation points, but is recurrently operative in the course of everyday life, in response to the smallest and most plebeian of stresses, and inherent in the ongoing process of unlearning and relearning that is so much a part of personal growth and our preparation for major life changes.

Disruption, for example: Your ten-year-old son fails to do his homework. You are angry and send him to his room to study right after dinner, not allowing him to watch his favorite television program. You hear his door slam. Climbing to the top of the stairs, you can hear him crying softly inside. You open the door and walk over to the bed where he is lying, tearfully peering through glasses at his schoolbook. As you put your arm around his shoulder, he first draws away, then nestles for a minute in your arms. Then he straightens up and asks you to leave so he can do his work. He's learned two things: that you love him, and that he must do his homework. You are reminded of your love for him and are reassured, within yourself, that discipline is part of being a good parent.

Every time we have to learn something important that goes against some presumption we previously held dear, disruption must occur. As one nineteen-year-old girl put it: "I thought I was a terrific athlete when I was in boarding school. I was the champion of our field hockey team. When I started college, I tried out for junior varsity. I remember sitting on the cold bench, waiting my turn. The girls trying out ahead of me looked like they belonged on the New York Giants football team. I felt like a fragile flower. No way could I compete with them. A small girls' school was one thing, but this! I was upset for weeks."

A thirty-five-year-old married woman told me this story. Her boss, a wealthy man in his early fifties and recently divorced, asked her to accompany him to an industry dinner. She wanted very much to go. There was only one problem: Her husband objected. She told him his jealousy was unfounded and irrational, but he only grew angrier. She asked herself whether she should give in to him and not go, even though she considered his behavior immature. Or should she insist on the innocence of the situation and go anyway, in spite of his feelings? Whichever choice she made, her relationship with her husband had been disrupted. If she gave in, she might resent his refusal to give her the right to make her own choices when, in her opinion, they didn't compromise her commitment to him. If she were to go anyway, what might happen afterward? Would he come to his senses and put the incident aside as insignificant? Would reconciliation restore closeness and encourage a new level of trust and respect? Or would a residue of hurt and distrust endure?

And then reintegration. The second part of the healthy response to stress involves putting the pieces of ourselves and our worlds together again into new homeostases. When a parent reassures his or her son after sending him to his room, although still insists that the homework be done, the self-esteem and confidence of both parent and son are strengthened. For the young woman who accepted the fact she would not make the varsity team, a new drive to succeed academically led her to graduate with highest honors. The woman who, in the end, decided to forfeit the opportunity to go out to dinner with her employer learned that she could compromise her wants without surrendering her autonomy, and her marriage grew stronger for it.

David Potter was a brilliant surgeon in his late fifties who found himself passing through the disruption-reintegration cycle. By the time he was fifty-eight, he had lost count of the number of coronary bypass operations he had performed. Most of his patients had lived and lived well. For years, every other Wednesday at ten, he donned his green pajamas and strode confidently down to the lecture room in the subbasement of the medical school to lecture on cardiovascular disease to the third-year medical students.

One evening, tired and discouraged about the lack of progress in a patient who did not seem to be recovering as he had expected, Dr. Potter spoke to his wife about their future. "I want to quit," he said. "I'm tired of malpractice insurance rates, bureaucracies, and petty academic jealousies and politics. I want to move out of town and live near the water, where I can enjoy life more."

Then he offered her a more substantial reason for his decision; his own physician had diagnosed the earliest stages of Parkinson's disease and it would no longer be possible for him to continue his surgical career.

They moved from New York City to Stonington, Connecticut, a small town on Long Island Sound. He continued as an adjunct professor at the medical school and went to New York once a month or so to lecture. He could become a consultant at a hospital in New Haven, where he could still involve himself with patients, although not in the operating room, and he would have more time for his favorite pastimes, sailing and doing watercolors.

However, the change was fraught with considerable turbulence. He and his wife had to forfeit many of the familiar landmarks of their lives, such as the practice of his highly developed skills, the home they had grown accustomed to, the convenience of having friends living nearby. David found himself with much more time on his hands than he had anticipated once he had departed from the rigorous routine to which he had grown accustomed. Many of the sources of his identification—his position at the medical center, colleagues with whom he worked every day, the students he taught—were gone, and he was faced with the need to construct a new identity within the framework of an unfamiliar lifestyle.

Shortly after the excitement and activity of the moving had subsided, David Potter found himself in a state of emotional distress. His usual zest and energy disappeared. He procrastinated about setting up his professional involvements in Connecticut. He grew depressed and irritable, often losing his temper with his wife about inconsequential things. Sleeping late into the mornings, he would spend an hour reading the newspaper over a ten o'clock breakfast and then disappear for several hours to walk aimlessly along the waterfront. He knew something was the matter. He had a vague notion that his problems were somehow connected with the changes in his life. Realizing he was not resolving the situation to his own satisfaction by himself, he spoke with me as an old friend and colleague.

Dr. Potter had many resources within himself to help him through such a crisis. Years of work had made him self-disciplined. He could not have become the professional he was without having learned how to postpone gratification and understanding the meaning of frustration, having been forced to deal with innumerable crises in the operating room. His normally wide range of interests was apparent, and his curiosity had compelled him to carry out quite a bit of original research in his field.

"What frightens me more than anything," he said, "is the fact that I seem to have lost confidence in myself for the first time in my life."

When I pointed out to him that his distress was a natural consequence of the changes in his. health and in the circumstances of his life, he was slightly puzzled. Dr. Potter had expected to adjust to these with his usual calm and deliberateness; when he found himself unable to do so without some degree of disabling tension, he was surprised and embarrassed, and he began to think less of himself for his seeming lack of determination. Then, giving it a second thought, he laughed. "We doctors aren't gods," he said, "even if we get used to doing the impossible sometimes."

Over the next few weeks, he felt his old familiar energy returning and set out to organize his new life according to the plan he had had in mind.

David Potter demonstrates our potential to reorganize ourselves and our lives after a period of stress, a capacity attributable to the fact that as human beings, we are "self-organizing systems." We have the capacity to restructure ourselves after disruption and achieve fresh, different, more meaningful levels of order and coherence, if we know how to activate it.

The law of psychobiological disruption and reintegration has serious import with regard to all of our lives:

- In order to learn and to experience meaningful change, we must fall apart.
- During periods of chaos, we are at varying degrees of risk, as we cannot determine in advance what direction our future will take.
- By making us more knowledgeable and adaptive, each period of disruption and reintegration is necessary to prepare us to meet the stresses that lie ahead.
- Failure to pass successfully through any stress cycle can leave us crippled, without the strengths we will need when other bifurcation points appear.

Nowhere, perhaps, are the challenges of chaos triggered by stress and the strength to survive it more vividly exemplified than in the experiences of men and women subjected to the trauma of terrible accidents or the enduring hardships of war. From their accounts we can begin to learn about resilience.

3

Survival

T
O DEEPEN my understanding of resilience, I decided to take a careful look at the recorded sources of strength that had enabled people exposed to some of the most dramatic conditions of stress imaginable to survive their time of chaos. The problems most of us face on a day-to-day basis may seem trivial (except to those of us involved in them) in comparison with sudden disasters or the awful circumstances of prisoner of war camps that so many men and women have endured. Nonetheless, the resilience that the survivors called upon to survive does not differ in substance from that which we require to deal with our own particular stresses.

Consider the aftereffects of traumatic situations that are sudden, unexpected, and short-lived, but that bring us face-to-face with disaster, death, and destruction, such as airplane and automobile crashes. Victims and even witnesses to such events are overwhelmed with confusion and terror. Those who are best able to reintegrate emotionally afterward have proved to be those given the chance to share their experiences verbally with each other and with understanding professionals.

I wish I had had this insight into the dynamics of survival

when I was twenty-three and felt I had all the time in the world stretching before me. I was a third-year medical student. Along with several of my classmates, I was spending the summer between my junior and senior years of medical school studying tropical medicine at the University of Havana, in Cuba. One bright, sunny afternoon, a friend and I took a small sailboat out from the Havana Yacht Club. In a brisk breeze, we carelessly sailed out much too far. We were not prepared for what happened. Although I had had a good deal of experience with boats, my friend had not. So when it came time to come about, he swung his body toward the wrong side of the boat. We capsized. The mast and sail floated away. With great effort, we were able to right the hull and crawl back into it. But it was filled with water up to our waists. Helpless, terrified, we sat there as the current drew us slowly along the coast. We knew we were too far from shore to swim; besides, the waters were filled with sharks.

All night long we sat there, watching the lights flicker off, one by one. A colorfully lit dance boat passed us by, but the loud music drowned out our cries for help. Then came total darkness. Hour after hour passed. I worried about how long the wooden shell would stay afloat and fought against the fear that we would die, either because the boat would sink or because we would drift out to sea and be scorched by the powerful tropical sun when day came. Sometime during the night, my friend cried out in pain; a large jellyfish, a Portuguese man-of-war, had swum across his abdomen, leaving in its wake painful welts produced by its poison. As I recall, he spoke of suicide and I, in desperation, encouraged us both to pray out loud.

Fourteen hours later—Did we fall asleep? Could we have? I can't remember—as dawn came, the sun rose in the distance above lush green hills that looked like a Vermont landscape. We were still the same distance from shore. The current had not carried us away! From the harbor in the province of Pinar del Río, we could see an old freighter slowly moving in our direction. As it came nearer, I could read a name painted on its side: Lehigh Portland Cement. Later, sitting on the deck of the rescue ship, drinking black coffee and biting on hard biscuits, I still shivered with fear.

We returned to New York and resumed our normal lives. I spoke superficially with a few friends about the experience, but never really expressed the feelings of terror, guilt, and remorse that had gripped me for so many hours at sea. I didn't sleep very well. I felt as though I had lost a precious sense of direction in my life. There were times when I felt as though I were floundering, and times when I actually felt strangely depressed. But I never connected these signs of stress to the accident until, several years later, I began my own personal psychoanalysis with Dr. Bertram Lewin as part of my preparation for psychiatric work. Then, for the first time, I released myself from these feelings of the past by sharing them and the full details of the experience with another human being.

Shell shock was the term used for it during the First World War, and later, *combat neurosis*. Most soldiers suffering with various forms of acute stress reactions in the context of combat reintegrated themselves quickly once they were removed from action and had the opportunity to talk about what they had been through. But for many, the memories and emotions connected with war continued to linger, sometimes revealing themselves through dreams, as if the unconscious mind was slowly, steadily resolving the psychological pain that had been inflicted. I recall a friend of mine who, when he was twenty-four years old, served with the British forces in China. Assigned as a military adviser to a Chinese infantry division, he and a few officers were separated from the main body of men when the Japanese attacked by surprise and in overwhelming numbers. He watched helplessly as heavy armor, supported by fighter planes and artillery, annihilated his comrades-in-arms. For hours, hidden in a nearby woods, trembling with fear, he could not move. Then, arduously, he and the few survivors found their way back to their command base. "Funny," he said to me once, "I don't remember being relieved at being alive. I don't remember feeling anything . . . except numbness. I never saw battle again. For years afterward, though, I had the same dream, over and over again. I'd be there, only a few hundred yards away, watching those troops being blown apart. Blood and the smell of death were everywhere. Then, a couple of years ago, the dream just disappeared."

During the Second World War and subsequent ones, prisoners of war were often forced to endure terrible stresses for years, especially where the terms of the Geneva Convention were ignored. Some stresses were climatic, others man-made. Torture, witnessing others being killed and being threatened with one's own death, humiliation, and starvation were common conditions, particularly in Japanese prison camps. Prisoners were exposed to extreme conditions of cold, as in Korea, and heat, as in Southeast Asia. They faced absolute rule by a hostile bureaucracy. They lived under conditions of severe overcrowding. Civilians and military alike were subject to destruction of values, status, society, and family, and to the continual threat of impending death. Prisoners hesitated to escape, even if the extremely rare opportunity for escape existed, for doing so would jeopardize the lives of fellow prisoners, some of whom might be summarily executed in reprisal.

Yet half of those exposed to such extreme conditions survived. What kind of coping mechanisms made the difference between life and death?

The most important survival factor was an obvious one, the will to live. However, this will to live depended strongly on two resilience traits we will explore in detail later on, the regulation of self-esteem and the endurance of hope. A psychiatrist, J. Nardini, who actually spent three and a half years in a Japanese prison camp after the fall of Bataan and Corregidor in 1942, expressed his formula for survival in this understated observation: "It was important to conceive of one's self as something better than the environment implied."

Those prisoners who had a purpose outside themselves in living—a cause to fight for, a family to return to—had a better chance of making it through. Within the severe limitations of prison life, the survivors seemed able to hold on to a sense of command over their environment. Psychologically they were able to remove themselves somewhat from the dehumanizing behavior of their captors. How?

Group affiliation helped enormously. By maintaining a semblance of military order among themselves and by reaching out to those who seemed to be in trouble—comrades who had surrendered psychologically, withdrawing into themselves and refusing to eat or communicate—they were able, in some measure, to counterbalance the destructive attitudes and actions of their common enemy. The extreme individualist was actually at greater risk than most.

Another vital component of survival was hope. On January 9, 1945, Lt. Henry G. Lee was killed when, ironically, the Japanese prison ship he was aboard was bombed off Formosa by planes from an American carrier. He had been held prisoner since his capture during the fall of Bataan in the Philippines. Written in a composition book, the kind we used in school as children, that was torn and covered with dirt, Lee's poems created during his years of confinement spoke of the hope that had helped keep him alive all through those dark times.

Lee wrote:

The right or wrong we cannot judge or know,
We only see that here a few must pay
A bitter penance, living day to day
And watching years unfold unused and slow.
We only feel our hungers wax and wane
To suit the whim that guides our captor's hate.
We only see the palsied hand of fate
Grope blindly on the tangled threads of pain
And leave this man untouched and that man dead.
We only feel the dream fade at the test,
The spirit quenched, the youth starved in the breast,
The heart grown calloused and the once-proud head
Bowed low beneath the captor's iron hand.
We only know our candle gleam of hope

Glows in a darkness where our minds must grope
Lost and forsaken, through a strange, gray land.

To some degree, hope is implanted in the earliest years of life, during the intimate relationship formed between parent and child, but it is invariably nurtured by all subsequent life experience that helps one develop a sense of one's own competence. Among prisoners of war, for example, younger soldiers, those between eighteen and twenty-two years old, with less soldiering and overall life experience, had a higher death rate than career servicemen, whose training and values enabled them to sustain long periods of hardship while retaining some measure of hope.

Hope is born of faith, the kind of faith that makes us believe that our lives serve an ultimate purpose in the scheme of things, that there is a higher power to whom we can turn in search of strength whenever we must pass through the "strange, gray land." Without it, the pain of disruption can indeed become unbearable.

4

The Strange, Gray Land

BIFURCATION POINTS, and even lesser moments of turmoil, are nearly always accompanied by emotional pain. Such pain is no less real than physical pain; it is often more intense, and often terrifying because it is commonly so difficult to describe or comprehend. Fear hurts. Anger hurts. So does despair—the sharp, acute despair that we might feel when a love relationship ends abruptly or someone close to us dies suddenly. Or there is the low-grade, incessant pain that may go on for months, or even years, when the life we have known has collapsed and we are stumbling in the dark in search of new structure and meaning.

Resilience depends on our ability to recognize pain, acknowledge its purpose, tolerate it for a reasonable time until things begin to take shape, and resolve our conflicts constructively. Managing emotional pain is more difficult than we might assume, calling for the survival strengths we have already noted, faith, hope, the will to live.

Unfortunately, many people try to ignore pain altogether, though at a very high price. Practicing the power of positive thinking is an inherently sound policy, but it can be carried too far, so that one fails to pay sufficient attention to the messages that pain may be trying to deliver. Imagine, for the moment, you had a case of appendicitis, but were able to shut out the pain. Regardless of how well you thought you felt, the infection would continue to spread throughout your body. If you did not seek treatment because you failed to recognize there was anything wrong, you could die.

By denying the reality of emotional pain, we may instead develop a variety of physical ailments that produce physical pain, from stomach ulcers to migraine headaches. In that event, we probably start a search for physical cures, but one that ultimately proves futile because our basic problems are not so much in our bodies as in our emotions.

Worse yet, we may turn to drugs to help us rid ourselves of pain—cocaine, for instance, or alcohol. Mark Hamilton was exhilarated when his film script about a rock and roll singer won wide acclaim and was nominated for an Academy Award. He had spent years of diligent effort to reach this point in his career, caddying at Palm Springs, waiting on tables at fashionable restaurants, driving a cab, while using the little spare time he could carve out to write. At thirty-five, he believed he had finally beaten the odds. Even though he had not actually won the Oscar, this recognition, so he thought, would assure him open doors and responsive producers for the storehouse of ideas he had been generating all those years.

To his surprise, nothing happened. His agent told him that the studios were afraid he would want too much money. Some who read his material felt it wasn't "commercial" enough. With bitterness, he saw a television movie one night that could have been lifted directly from one of his stories. In the credits was the name of a production house that had rejected his scripts. He was offered the chance to doctor the scripts of others, a job that didn't pay badly. He took it, but hated each new assignment more than the one that had preceded it. Once, when he persuaded a studio executive to read a treatment he had been working on, "the man," as he was called, took out his cigarette lighter and set fire to the manuscript in front of Mark, dropping it into a metal wastebasket.

He reminded Mark that even though he had been nominated for the statue, he hadn't won it.

That day was the first time Mark drank a double Scotch at lunch. It felt warm and soothing. It took away the pain. By the time he joined Alcoholics Anonymous three years later, he and his wife were divorced, and she had moved back to Rhode Island with their two children. He had been unable to write for over two years. To earn a few dollars, he sold Toyotas.

I met Mark at a meeting of Alcoholics Anonymous, where I had been invited to give a lecture.

"I've been off the stuff for six months," he told me, "but I still can't shake the paralysis. I can't write. I can't even think of stories to write about. When I try, all I can put down on paper is hate. And I can't get rid of this terrible pressure, here, in the center of my chest."

Nothing in Mark's background could have predicted how he would have handled his "strange, gray land," months that stretched into years, filled with loneliness, abuse, loss, and desperation. It had all come on him at the very moment he had become convinced that his efforts and his dedication to his talent had finally begun to pay off.

"It's like climbing Mount Everest," he said. "You reach the first level and you feel wonderful and you know you have the drive and energy to go on to the next. Then, suddenly, you fall off the mountain, or more precisely, a whole lot of people gang up to shove you off."

"You must have known the kind of business you were in," I said.

"Sure. But you believe that once you make it . . . Besides, nobody thinks it will happen to them."

"And you know what it takes to go on, to succeed again."

"I can spell it out for you. Patience. Guts. Endurance. Resourcefulness."

I asked him what had happened to his.

"I was taken off guard. I couldn't stand the pain and humiliation."

"That's why you drank?"

"It helped me forget. It got me to sleep. In the end, I drank because I drank."

By using alcohol to relieve his pain, Mark Hamilton had drained whatever resilience he might otherwise have had. At the same time, he kept both himself and his world in a continuing state of imbalance. He had not really been prepared for what had happened. In the beginning, he had seen himself as a hardworking young artist, willing to take any menial job to make a living while struggling to create. It was quite an acceptable self-image. Young. Just married. A child on the way. Banging away on his typewriter. As assistant manager of a local supermarket, cheerfully waving his paycheck in front of his wife when he arrived home at the end of the first week on the job. It was fun.

But the real test was yet to come.

Being thirty-six, having received a taste of recognition, having been looked on—or so he thought—as a serious writer, he was totally unprepared for the ignominious neglect and outright abuse he was about to face. Nothing in his philosophy of life or expectations of himself and the world enabled him to anticipate or deal with the frustrations he was to encounter and the consequent pain he would experience. He had been born and brought up in the second half of the twentieth century in Scarsdale, New York, of upper-middle-class parents. Mark's great disappointments in the past had consisted in his father's working so hard to maintain the family's style of living that he had very little time left over to sail or go on outings with his children, and his not being taken to Tavern on the Green, an expensive New York restaurant, for his thirteenth birthday, as so many of his school friends had been.

Now he was faced with learning the hard way the meaning of courage, self-discipline, and realistic hope. I could only hope he would.

There are several good reasons why experienced psychiatrists generally prefer not to use medications too liberally to remove psychological pain. With the premature removal of pain, one's motivation for change is often reduced. A second reason is that by observing the triggers for pain, it is possible for a person to find previously hidden or unrecognized sources of distress within his or her own makeup or life situation. This is not unlike the physician's carrying out a physical examination and going back over an area of the body again and again to identify the exact location and, hence, the nature of a reported pain. Often, at first, turmoil will appear to be all-encompassing. On the other hand, you may be convinced that one part of your life is the primary source of your difficulty—your marriage, for example—when the real culprit lies elsewhere—perhaps in your career. It is important to watch for clues that link pain to its real origins.

One of the most important reasons, however, for not deadening emotional pain prematurely is to enable the required time to pass and the necessary insight to be gained that will permit you, during and after a period of disruption, to put the pieces together again into a fresh and better whole. Otherwise, one can easily resume old, unaltered patterns of behavior or continue living in a situation without making important and needed improvements.

There are three important tactics that many people I know, including myself, have used to alleviate emotional pain. The first is diversion—to remove ourselves mentally or geographically from destructive, devitalizing influences within us or around us to find temporary sanctuary, a response not unlike the answer to battle fatigue. During and following a period of prolonged stress, I can literally feel the tension flow out of my body as the plane takes off en route to some faraway place and I leave the cares and responsibilities I have been struggling with behind me for a while. If I am wrestling with an especially distressing situation, I try to discipline myself not to dwell on its particulars over and over again, in thought or conversation. Rather, I seek to find stimulation in the form of reading, films, a brisk walk, contact with others—anything sufficiently diverting to draw my attention away from wounds that may be festering, so that they have a chance to heal, or from problems that for the moment seem unsolvable, so that I can come upon unexpected answers farther down the road.

The second tactic involves self-discipline and control. One of the most painful aspects of periods of disruption is the feeling of having lost control, over oneself or over one's life. It can indeed be terrifying. Your husband or wife has asked you in no uncertain terms for a divorce. Your child lies suffering in a nearby hospital, being treated for severe burns. Along with ten thousand others in your company, you've been laid off in a cost-cutting effort after twenty years of employment. These are representative events you cannot control. It may or may not be too late to rehabilitate your marriage. Your child must be left to the professionals, and there is nothing you can do. There is no way to influence and reverse the corporate decision, made by a group of anonymous faces in some boardroom somewhere. What I commonly advise people to do at such times is to attend to those matters that are still under their command, concentrating on what they are able to do, while letting what they cannot influence run its natural course.

Television commercials promise us innumerable ways to make life easy and success quick, from cooking a frozen gourmet dinner in five minutes to becoming a millionaire in eighteen months by buying real estate with no money down. Self-discipline has become something of a lost art. Fred Astaire was known to have practiced his original dance routines again and again to perfect them. By the time his film had been edited and we, the audience, had the pleasure of watching the finished version in the movie house, he appeared to move effortlessly across the stage. It looked so simple. But it wasn't. Thomas Edison, who some of us may imagine simply thought up new ideas and had them built, once remarked that "invention is one percent inspiration and ninety-nine percent perspiration." What applies to dancing, art, athletics, scientific invention, and brain surgery applies no less to the game of life. Self-discipline is a critical attribute of resilience, and something we learn best through practice.

The third tactic involves empathy. There is perhaps no more effective way to relieve psychic pain than to be in contact with another human being who understands what you are going through and can communicate such understanding to you. In looking for empathy, you will have to keep in mind that there is no perfect empathizer; one friend may understand certain aspects of your life that others won't. Furthermore, you must be selective in whom you turn to for empathy. Don't look for it where it cannot be found. Some people seem singularly incapable of any empathy at all, and turning to such a person in time of need can only make you hurt that much more.

I recall once meeting a woman in her late thirties at a dinner party, who told the story of her husband's suicide. "He was very depressed, although I don't know what about. I certainly didn't give him anything to be upset about. Maybe he had business problems, or problems with his children by his other marriage. He just didn't have the guts to face life. If I'd known what a weak person he was, I would never have married him."

I asked her when the tragedy had occurred.

"Three weeks ago," she said. Then, smiling, she added: "You can't grieve forever."

I trembled, envisioning her husband looking at her for one small measure of empathy that might have eased his pain and, not finding it, feeling compelled to end his suffering the only way he could think of in his troubled state of mind.

We would all do well to appraise the people in our lives in advance of crises and figure out whom we can turn to in need. We'd also do well to ask ourselves how capable we are of empathy when someone who needs us turns to us for help.

5

A New Definition of
Mental Health

PSYCHIATRISTS have always struggled with the attempt to define normality, and it remains the subject of heated debate. Some embrace the perspective in which you and I are considered to be normal as long as we manifest no obvious pathology, as set down in a strict, standard glossary of definitions provided by the *Diagnostic Statistical Manual* of the American Psychiatric Association. If we can operate in a more or less rational way on a day-to-day basis, free of unreasonable psychic pain, discomfort, or disability, we are presumed to be all right.

According to another perspective, normality implies a harmonious blending of the many diverse aspects of our personality so that we are optimally engaged in something called self-actualization. We are always becoming more, incessantly gaining in self-knowledge. Of course, as total self-knowledge is inherently an impossibility, those who hold to this point of view are forced to admit that there can really be no completely developed and hence "normal" person.

A third school of thought defines normality as a total lack of imagination, conformity to one's environment without attempting to change it, and psychological inflexibility. Those adhering to this definition are quite serious about this, although the definition is not, nor was it meant to be, flattering. It is based on the idea of normal as a statistical average. Its advocates look at human behavior in the context of the bell curve of distribution. Most of us fall underneath the central, high point of the curve. Deviations from this point in either direction begin to constitute uniqueness and maladaptation. It seems to me that if this is a form of normality, it can ensure health only if you are fortunate to live a life of very uninteresting times indeed.

The fourth prominent definition of normality stresses that it is the result of interacting systems that change over time and can be understood only when viewed from a standpoint of temporal progression. This perspective corresponds most closely with my own, at least to the degree that it involves the concept of homeostatic structures and the phenomenon of change. However, many of its adherents believe that when a system collapses, illness is the necessary result.

In fact, all four perspectives take a dim view of falling apart, especially if such an event is associated with any degree of intense emotional pain or disability. Ironically, it is exactly disruption, and most commonly a period of dysfunction, that often constitutes a truly healthy response to meaningful stress, whether occurring concurrently with such stress or after the immediate threat has subsided. As I view it, it is not the disruption that is the illness. Instead, disease is the failure to disrupt when disruption is called for, and the failure to reintegrate afterward to form a new synthesis.

I do not mean to imply that whenever we're subjected to major stresses, we must fall apart extensively. Quite the contrary. While a serious and temporarily incapacitating collapse may reflect a healthy response to such events rather than illness, ideal conditions of resilience will usually enable us to maintain some degree of equilibrium and weather most episodes of disruption without such severe consequences.

These two options for illness are shown in Figures 2 and 3. Traditional psychiatric diagnoses have long acknowledged the

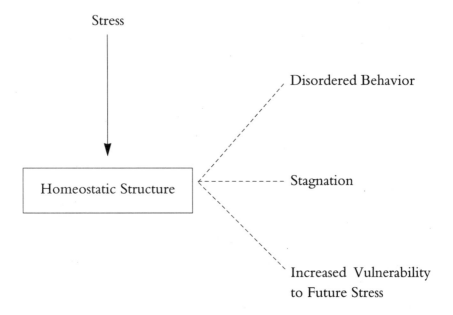

Figure 2. *Illness Option A: The Failure to Disrupt*

relationship between phases in the life cycle and the occurrence of illness. It is a well-known fact that emotional disorders cluster around transitional stages in the life cycle. Adolescence is often a time that triggers what have been called the schizophrenias. A host of so-called neurotic disorders, ranging from psychosomatic illnesses, such as duodenal ulcers, to phobic states, make their appearance during the early and mid-twenties. The incidence of depression has been shown to be particularly high among women in their early thirties, and more so among mothers with three or more children under the age of five. Postpartum depression, from the "baby blues" to full-blown illness, is a well-known phenomenon. The term *involutional melancholia* was once used to describe profound depression in someone being overwhelmed by the challenges of middle age, and suicide is extremely common among the elderly, especially if they live alone or are physically unwell.

What has rarely been acknowledged, until now, is that so-called nervous breakdowns, rather than reflecting illness as such,

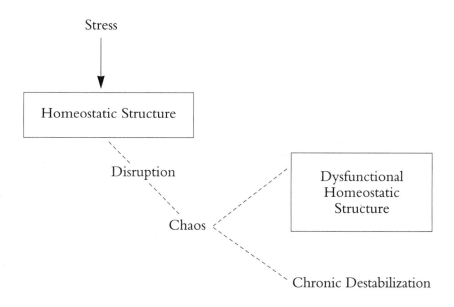

Figure 3. *Illness Option B: The Failure to Reintegrate Successfully*

may be manifestations of the normal disruption that accompanies these transition periods or, as is often the case, an intensified form of such disruption, one that may at times assume catastrophic proportions because earlier transitions in the life cycle were not successfully accomplished.

Consider Jim Bourne's story, for example. During the first twenty-two years of Jim Bourne's life, one could say that he was well put together, living in an environment essentially conducive to a healthy and constructive life development. The elder of two children born to upper-middle-class parents, he grew up in a small town in Maryland, just outside Washington, D.C. He graduated first in his high school class, and attended Georgetown University, where he majored in English and also graduated with honors. He was popular, socially outgoing, quite confident of himself. Only his lack of athletic prowess caused him some grief; but even that did not trouble him greatly, so obvious were his accomplishments elsewhere. He then went on to earn a master's in business administration at the Wharton School, in Philadelphia. While he was a student there, he met and married his wife, Grace. She was his first serious love, and he did not take the time or make the effort to try his hand at a variety of relationships before making this important life choice.

He was twenty-five when he first consulted me. He had recently entered a training program at a prestigious investment banking firm in New York. Well mannered, articulate, orderly in his thinking and conversation, he was, nonetheless, quite uncomfortable with the predicament in which he found himself. He struggled to avoid crying in front of me. His complaint was exhaustion, but it might as easily have been humiliation. I was struck by the fact that this obviously accomplished person appeared to have little or no confidence left in himself.

Jim's wife was originally from New York. She was the daughter of a wealthy industrialist, presumably attractive (I never met her), with a rather strong disposition (more like Jim's father than his quiet reserved mother). I gathered, from what he told me, that he and Grace were frequently mentioned in the social columns. They lived in a town house on Sutton Place, purchased with his wife's financial help.

It didn't take long for me to determine that Jim felt dwarfed by his new in-laws and all they represented to him. His own achievements suddenly seemed inconsequential by comparison. Even though he was in a line of work that, if he were successful, promised him the chance to become wealthy himself, it was not what he felt cut out to do.

"I can do the work. I'm not stupid. But I don't want to spend my life putting together financing for large corporations. It doesn't seem enough. There's an old saying, 'You only come this way once.' I want to do something with meaning."

Jim had originally wanted to be a writer. He had thought sometimes of becoming the publisher of a newspaper. Sometimes he had considered being a minister, like his mother's brother, Uncle Adam. But during his last year in college, he was swept up in the race to go to graduate school. Not wanting to be a doctor or lawyer, he chose business instead. He'd been offered a job with a newspaper in Saint Petersburg, Florida, after graduation. But his new wife wanted to live in New York, where his efforts to obtain a position with a newspaper proved futile. On his own, without the aid of her family connections, he secured his job in the financial world.

Within the framework of his new environment, Jim seemed to have lost a good deal of the independence of spirit he had once possessed. His ambitions and his working situation appeared mismatched. Pulled more and more into his wife's orbit, he had forfeited many of his own interests and practically all of his old friends. He lived a life one might describe as a state of quiet desperation that he himself did not truly comprehend.

He described his relationship with Grace as "solid." "We never argue. There's nothing to argue about. True, she shapes the kind of personal life we lead, but that's okay with me." (I didn't entirely believe him.) "On our wedding trip, we laughed about the idea that we were like an old married couple who had been together for years." Grace was proud of his job. Whenever he tried to talk with her about changing his career direction, she would smile and bury the issue with a dozen concerns about everyday matters such as dinner parties and weekends with her family in the country.

Clearly, Jim was afraid of losing control over himself. The distress he felt—which he attributed to being overwhelmed by the amount of work involved in his current projects—frightened him. At first, he experienced pounding sensations in his chest, especially in the middle of the night; he thought he might be suffering with heart disease. But his physician quickly disabused him of this notion and suggested he consult me.

He must have found our few visits enormously reassuring, for by the third, he was already feeling better. I suggested psychoanalysis, in those early days of my career considering it an appropriate regimen for him. He refused, and thanked me for being a good listener and for helping him accept his situation. "It's not exactly a bad one, you know," he felt.

The next time I saw Jim Bourne was in the emergency room of the New York Hospital fourteen years later. He had been brought by ambulance after threatening to commit suicide. He appeared much older. He had obviously lost quite a bit of weight and seemed a shadow of the bright young man I recalled having met years earlier. Trembling, avoiding my glance, wearing a pair of striped pajamas and a light-blue bathrobe, he sat in a straight-back plastic chair, his hands clenched together, staring into space.

It seemed that Jim had been increasingly depressed for nearly a year, as he approached his fortieth birthday. He again suffered with grave doubts about his career; for apparently political reasons, he had not been promoted to a senior level at his firm. About two years before, his second child, a son (he and Grace had three altogether) had fallen from a horse in Martha's Vineyard, where the family spent the summers; the boy's optic nerve had been severed in the fall, and he would be blind for life. Thereafter, for the first time in their marriage he and his wife began to argue. She accused him of having affairs (which he did not), of drinking too much and being alcoholic (clearly not correct), and of having become a selfish and unfeeling man (no doubt partly true).

One evening, after a dinner party, Grace insisted on driving home, complaining that Jim had had too much to drink. On the way, the car skidded on an ice patch. She lost control. In the ambulance on the way to the hospital, the volunteer rescue worker told Jim that she had been killed. Three months later, gripped with despair and guilt, feeling that his whole world had collapsed, and completely losing all perspective, Jim tried to end his own life.

Now, fourteen years after our first meeting, I saw Jim Bourne going through another period of disruption, this time quite profound; for, in stark contrast to his episode of falling apart at age twenty-five, when the world around him remained intact, this time its structure had come apart too. Grace's family, holding him responsible for her death, were openly hostile toward him. Having cut himself off from most of the friends from his earlier life and having become extremely, almost exclusively, dependent on

Grace—a dependence that had been threatened by the growing tension between them—he found himself entirely alone, except for his children, at his moment of crisis. Moreover, as before, he was extremely humiliated by his helplessness and lost all respect for himself.

Because I could not be sure how serious a suicide risk he represented, I felt it essential to hospitalize him. He remained in the hospital for twelve weeks. There, in addition to psychotherapy, he received antidepressant medication. I was amazed at how quickly he rebounded. With unusual speed, he engaged in reformulating his life pattern, making plans that he would put into execution after discharge. Over the months that followed, he made a concerted effort to contact old friends. His breakdown had made him persona non grata at his firm; they did not actually fire him, but they made it painfully obvious that they would welcome his resignation. He offered it to them with a certain bravado, although he could not entirely conceal his hurt at their rejection and lack of understanding. Together with an old friend from business school days, he started a videocassette distribution company in Boston, which subsequently proved to be very profitable. He bought a house in Newburyport, up the coast, hired a housekeeper, and began to spend most of his free time with his children.

I didn't see Jim again until another seven years had gone by. He was forty-six. He had recently married again and felt he was having some trouble adjusting to some of the conditions of his new life situation; he wanted some guidance in handling some day-to-day issues that had arisen. "I'm slightly down," he admitted. Then, smiling, he added: "But I'm not embarrassed to be." He described the problems. "Giving up my independence a second time hasn't been easy. I don't like conflicts, but I've been trying a new approach to my relationships with everyone, by being up-front, saying what I feel, without being undiplomatic, of course . . . except, maybe, when I lose my temper. The children seem to love her, but I've found myself pulled between her and them . . . and maybe Grace's memory."

We spoke of the past.

"After my breakdown, it was as though I was back in touch with the person I'd been as a young man. More confident. I missed Grace for a long time, but I learned to be on my own. Even my sense of humor returned. It was terrifying at the time, being so out of control. I've forgiven myself. I found a new sense of myself that you can probably only discover by overcoming terrible adversities, just like they say."

Was Jim Bourne ill? I believe so. But it was not the illness that current diagnostic criteria would have given him. The serious episode of depression would have been labeled, for the record, a major affective disorder. Because of his earlier bout with mild depression, some of my colleagues might classify his as a recurrent type of depression. Because of his professional success, some might even suspect a subtle bipolar, or, as it used to be called, manic-depressive disorder. Whatever value such terms may have in focusing treatment measures or in the evaluation of research investigations—and it is both a real and a relevant value—I believe that they seriously misstate the issue.

And it is an important issue. For how we experience episodes of disruption, and how those around us view what we are experiencing, can profoundly influence our success in dealing with stress and the eventual outcome of our struggle.

Jim's first serious bifurcation point occurred when he was twenty-five. Something within him was trying to tell him that things weren't quite the way they should be. For a variety of reasons, including the fact that his external environment remained steadfastly intact at that time, Jim pulled himself together very quickly—too quickly, in fact, and quite inadequately, as he failed to make the needed changes in himself or his world. He might have learned to become more independent and, hence, might not have been so catastrophically affected by Grace's death. He might have cultivated friends of his own, some of whom might have served him well in his time of need. He might have realized how important his children were to him and he to them, an appreciation that has deterred many from seriously considering suicide in moments of despair.

These were the opportunities he passed by, and by doing so, he failed to cope successfully with his critical bifurcation point. His real diagnosis, then, might well have been termed premature pseudointegration, or bifurcation failure. Most significantly, his ineptness left him with serious unfinished business that only rendered him that much more vulnerable to the catastrophic stresses that awaited him at age thirty-nine.

I could not have predicted the outcome for Jim Bourne as we sat in the hospital emergency room that night. I only knew that everything in his life had come apart. His grief for his wife and his guilt over the circumstances of her death, the strains of having a disabled child, and the stresses of impending middle age with his own personal career confusion, combined with the unfinished business of his earlier failure to reintegrate successfully, caused a veritable psychological explosion.

What might his real diagnosis have been at that point in time? Considering what was happening, certainly not just the fact that he was depressed. After all, wouldn't some degree of falling apart seem a most logical and even healthy response to such overwhelming circumstances?

The fact is, at that moment, I couldn't make what I considered an accurate diagnosis. It was what would happen later that would permit me to do so. The success of his reintegration during a short period of hospitalization and his ability to carve out a new and meaningful life for himself afterward convinced me that from a psychological point of view, he deserved no diagnosis as such at all. He did require antidepressant medication, which I interpret as evidence that at a biological level, whatever biochemical activity one needs to recover from a state of serious disruption wasn't working as well as it should have. Hence, in search of a diagnosis, I would be forced to invent some such phrase as "biochemical restorative insufficiency" or "clogged response systems."

Jim Bourne does illustrate several special, important points about the disruption-reintegration cycle and its relevance to mental health. It may take a great deal of stress to affect some people who are very tightly organized, especially if they also are living in highly structured environments. Moreover, the failure to pass successfully through any bifurcation point will leave most of us terribly vulnerable to the impact of subsequent stresses, whatever they may be.

His story also illustrates the great importance of doing as little harm as possible to the patients you are treating (if you are a physician) or the friends you are trying to help (if you are a friend). One of medicine's oldest adages is *Noli nocere,* which means "In the effort to heal, do no injury." When Jim first consulted me as a young man, he thought he was on the verge of a "nervous breakdown" or worse. Consequently, he postponed his initial consultation for a long time, and once he sought help, he fled the chance to learn through therapy as quickly as he could, in no small measure because he believed that by so doing he could obliterate the humiliation he felt for being "sick." I must admit that, at that stage of my thinking, I probably contributed to his dilemma by regarding him as suffering with a diagnosable psychiatric disorder and, hence, could not reassure him with proper confidence that he was not.

Although his second bout with stress-induced disruption was far more dramatic, this time I was able to share with him my then new perspective about what he was experiencing. Once he realized that his collapse was not a sign of mental illness per se, but that it was all right, if not essential, to fall apart under the conditions in which he found himself, his attitude toward himself improved and his motivation to recover was sharply enhanced. Unfortunately, many of his former associates and acquaintances failed to share this vision; consequently, some went out of their way to avoid him, while others regarded him as if he were a permanent cripple. On the other hand, as that more or less forced him to seek new friendships and another lifestyle, perhaps their aversion wasn't such a misfortune after all.

Basically, I do not believe that we can continue to define mental health in such simplistic terms as the ability to survive the impact of stressful events, particularly the stress associated with bifurcation points, without falling apart. Quite the contrary. The healthy response often involves such falling apart, and failure to do so is the illness, even as illness exists if we cannot put ourselves and the pieces of our lives together again in a new, more effective synthesis afterward.

I have termed the strengths we require to master cycles of disruption and reintegration throughout our lives *resilience;* and it is resilience that is at the heart of what we call mental health.

PART II

The Life Cycle

6

Transiting the Life Cycle

THE HUMAN LIFE CYCLE presents us with a series of homeostatic structures that extend from birth to old age, separated from each other by bifurcation points. From childhood to adolescence; from adolescence to young adulthood; from being single to being married and then being a parent, or adjusting to life alone; from being a young family, planning and full of hope, to reaching middle age, career peaking, children grown and gone; from retirement to old age—each stage in life has special characteristics, responsibilities, opportunities, that require us to change in order to cope with them effectively. Movement from one stage to another inevitably induces some measure of upheaval as we are pulled between the forces of past and future, dismantling one homeostatic structure so as to set the stage for the creation of a new and different one.

These are predictable shifts, although we see a good deal of variability in how each of us will be affected by and cope with them. Moreover, unpredictable disruptive incidents also occur, wildly unexpected events that can change the course of one's entire future.

As we struggle, caught in the tug-of-war between maintaining existing structures within ourselves and our worlds while, at the same time, responding to the compelling need for change, some degree of chaos is a critical part of giving up attitudes and patterns of behavior by which we have come to define ourselves, but which have grown outmoded, even harmful; yet this is an absolute requirement if we are to meet the demands and explore the dimensions of the stage in life that lies before us.

The bifurcation points that separate one stage in the life cycle from the next are not destined to occur at one particular age. They may begin earlier in one person, later in another. They are not necessarily well circumscribed in time: For one person, the phase of instability may take place over a period of months; for another, it may stretch out over several years. Nor will each bifurcation point assume the same intensity in all people. One person may weather the vicissitudes of adolescence with a minimum of distress, but arrive at middle age to find himself in great turmoil. Another may flounder from the time he is twelve years old until he is married and settled into a career, but thereafter find that as he moves toward middle age and beyond, subsequent bifurcation points are relatively benign.

Eight homeostatic structures appear in sequence (or parallel) during the normal life cycle: (1) childhood, (2) adolescence, (3) young, single adulthood, (4) young marriage, (5) parenthood, (6) single life, (7) middle age, and (8) aging. These are illustrated in the following diagram, which also highlights the six bifurcation points that lie between them.

Although the actual conditions of each of life's stages differ materially from those of others, there are certain universal issues that recur each time we pass through a bifurcation point.

- The need to adapt to changing external circumstances
- Reconsideration of one's self-image, and holding on to and restoring self-esteem
- Forming new human relationships and renewing old ones
- Giving up people and things we love because they die or go away

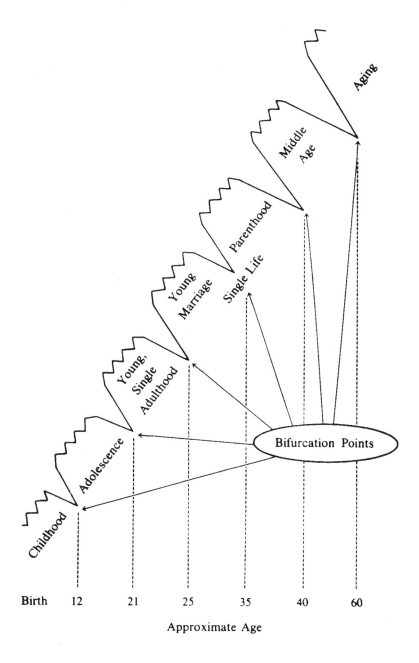

Figure 4. *Life Cycle Stages: Homeostatic Structures*

- Balancing our ability to be independent against our need for others
- Redefining or reaffirming our purposes in life

The amount of emphasis each of these objectives will receive will vary in different individuals living under different life circumstances at different stages in the life cycle, a fact that will become apparent as we examine more closely the stages themselves and the bifurcation points that lead us from one to the next.

7

Arrivals and Departures

Childhood

Nature has generously prolonged the childhood of human beings to provide us with a substantial period of time to learn what we require for personal survival as well as that of our species. Beginning with the disruptive experience of birth itself, the child confronts innumerable adaptational demands that, for him, are quite original and insist on a high degree of flexibility and creativity. To realize that he is not a symbiotic part of his mother, but an individual unto himself, is the first serious consideration of his own self-image. As she comes and goes, into his room and out of it, and as he gains confidence that even though she is no longer in sight she is still somewhere about and will return, he is engaged in his first experiment with adapting to changing circumstances. Contact with father, then perhaps brothers and sisters, and even household help and baby-sitters, starts the process of forming new human relationships, an experience upon which he must expand as he encounters neighborhood children, their parents, other adults, and teachers and little boys and girls in preschool classes.

He is always giving up something—the exclusive involvement

with his mother, the comfortable safety of his room and home, the tiny-tot toys that once thrilled his curiosity but are now outgrown, the friends he played with in kindergarten who have moved away, and, perhaps, a grandparent who has died. After he's been punished for being naughty or felt embarrassed because he could not do something that all the other children at school seemed able to do, he must learn to regain self-respect. From the time he begins to crawl, then walk, then run, and from the time he learns to read for himself rather than depending entirely on others to read for him, he is immersed in a series of exercises designed to encourage autonomy; yet there is, ideally, always someone to turn to when he hurts, hold his hand when he stumbles, explain the meaning of a word he does not understand.

Nowhere, perhaps, is the shifting from one internal homeostatic structure to another as obvious as during this phase in the life cycle. As he proceeds from infancy to becoming a toddler and then on to later childhood, the child experiences dramatic, successive movement from one level of adaptation to the next. There is a steady emergence of coping abilities and personality structure as he learns to identify who and what he is, how to communicate using language, how to think in concepts, how to acquire a sense of competence to deal with the world, and how to adapt to various changing circumstances. His knowledge— and, most importantly, his capacity for knowing—increases with each stage in his development. He is repeatedly trading off one psychological homeostatic state for another on his way to finally forming a personality structure that will serve to meet the challenges of his adult years.

It is remarkable how smoothly and adeptly most healthy children make these transitions, interrupting their passages with an occasional cry, a reaching for the favorite blanket they once cherished, an outburst of temper, a transient reluctance to go to school, hanging on to a parent's hand before letting go to rush on, upstairs, to a strange new classroom. Their suppleness and flexibility speak for themselves. At the same time, it is no surprise that their success in these ventures depends in no small measure on an environment that is consistent, more or less predictable, protective, and caring.

In so many ways, the growing child is the master of transition, the prototype of what we will later explore as resilience. Imaginative, responsive, observant, he is eager to relate to the world around him, and his recovery time from disappointment and frustration is often quick and full of new learning.

Studies of what children experience show clearly that each step of their development—from following moving objects with their eyes to gaining confidence in their ability to perform somersaults, from engaging other children in competition and play to mastering the composition of sentences—is essential as a preparation for the challenges that lie ahead. Should they fail to pass successfully through any critical phase or be unable to meet important challenges, they risk being limited—sometimes reversibly, sometimes not—in the ability to fulfill their future potential. In fact, such failure so early in life can have severe consequences indeed, misshaping much of what will be learned and experienced in years to come.

Archie Madden was seventeen when he took his scholastic aptitude test for college admission and succeeded in earning what may well have been the lowest score in the test's history. At the private day school Archie attended, he was anything but a scholar. His grade average was C+, with an occasional B. Because he wrote exceptional poetry and demonstrated a good deal of originality in his photography, most of his teachers were bewildered by his academic ineptness—all but one, his history teacher. He understood what Archie's problem was, where it came from, and, to some degree, how to be of help.

When the boy was four years old, he lost the hearing in his right ear as a result of a childhood infectious disease. However, this deficit was not detected until he was nearly eight, in the third grade. For almost four years in school, Archie had often perceived what was being said in segments; as he turned his head in one direction or another, his teacher's voice would fade in and out, like when the volume on a radio is turned up and down. Having no frame of reference for what he was experiencing, Archie himself assumed that this was the way hearing worked, and only when he was seven and a half could he accurately describe it so as to obtain a diagnosis and adequate correction. He was given a hearing aid and a seat in the front of the class. By then, of course, he had missed out on many aspects of the normal development of language that he could easily have mastered had he not been handicapped.

His teachers assumed that now that the problem had been solved, Archie should suddenly perk up and do better work. What they failed to appreciate was that simply treating his deafness was not enough to make up for the learning deficits that had occurred during the three vital years when the problem had eluded recognition. Moreover, during that time, Archie himself assumed—as many children would—that how he heard what he heard was perfectly normal. Hence, he adapted his thinking to a style that seemed somewhat disorganized and seriously impeded his later performance in school.

Fortunately, the perceptive teacher in high school who chose to be Archie's mentor understood this well. He took the boy aside several hours each week, carefully going over the principles of language and composition with him, retraining him gradually and persistently to think and express himself in more logical fashion. Of course, he knew there wasn't time to do the entire job while Archie was still under his tutelage, but he also had confidence that once the boy understood what was required, self-healing could begin and he could, on his own over a period of years, make up for what he had missed during his childhood development. Moreover, with this teacher's guidance and strong recommendation, Archie matriculated in a fine college, where creativity was valued and test scores viewed with a healthy level of skepticism. Last year, Archie Madden completed his thesis for and was awarded his Ph.D. in history.

Archie also demonstrates how resilient a child can be when confronted with serious stress. Doing so poorly in school hardly enhanced his self-esteem. He was embarrassed to bring his report cards home for his parents' signature, but, being honest and courageous, he did so nonetheless. His father was a renowned biologist. Archie very much wanted to emulate him, but by the time he was ten, he felt that such a career was beyond his reach. Abandoning this hope made him feel despondent at times. How, then, did this sensitive and inherently intelligent child deal with his disappointment and regain self-esteem? Intuitively, he turned to one of his vital strengths, his visual talents. For his eleventh birthday, his parents bought him a fine camera, and he mastered its use. He began to experiment with poetry, a form of expression involving imagery in which he became more than a little proficient. And he sought another source of self-worth in his relationships with his friends at school, where he was known for his loyalty and caring.

Entering Adolescence: The First Bifurcation Point

By the time most of us reach the brink of adolescence, our personalities are more or less formed, for better or worse. We now possess an internal structure that, although it will continue to be modified by future education and various life experiences, also has strong homeostatic power and resists change as we encounter stress caused by the struggle between what we are and what we are about to become, between unlearning what has become obsolete—how to be a successful child, for example—and learning something quite new—such as how to become adult.

There is an ancient Chinese saying, "May you live in interesting times." On the surface, it sounds like a very nice sentiment. But it has, like many such sayings, a less-apparent implication—for interesting times are really quite dangerous times.

Adolescence is an "interesting time." It is full of risk. For most of us, in fact, it is the first truly major bifurcation point, if it has not been preceded by an unexpected disrupting event, such as divorce in the family or a parent's death. Besides pulling away from childhood and the safe role you have occupied within your family, which gave you meaning, you are searching for new meaning, experimenting with the adventures of learning, new relationships, your whole future. The excitement of all this is intermingled with natural self-doubt and moments of sincere grief. Disruption and reintegration are indeed the business of the day.

There are four main events, or objectives, with which the adolescent must come to terms during this enormously important period of life, which, in so many ways, sets the stage for much that will follow.

- *The experience of loss as we say good-bye to the persons we were and to the familiar conditions of childhood:*

Alice Frohm lay in her bed, unable to fall asleep, thoughts rushing through her mind. She had spent the entire evening studying for her history test. Even though she always did well, she always worried too. She went over again the critical dates of the American Revolution, one by one, on the fingers of her hand. Then her mind drifted onto her twelfth birthday, coming up in three weeks. Who would she invite to her party? What kind of cake did she want? No more stuffed animals, she had told her mother. Maybe a pair of earrings. Beside her, on her pillow, lay her favorite friend, a soft, brown bear. She reached for it and cuddled it.

Because Alice had two older sisters, she knew what to expect soon. In one way, she was looking ahead to becoming really grown up. In another way, it all sounded a bit of a nuisance. A couple of girls in her class had already matured, and all they seemed to talk about was going to dances and boys. Alice thought that seemed stupid.

Then, unexpectedly, she felt tears in her eyes. She wiped them away.

Through the wall that separated her room from her parents', she could hear the eleven o'clock news on television. Her father must be in bed watching it. Slowly she lifted herself up, swung both feet onto the floor, and groped to find her slippers. Then, tiptoeing out into the hall and seeing the light on in the other room, she knocked gently and asked if she could come in. Her father was lying there, as she knew he would be, propped up against his three pillows. She lay on the bed next to him, asking if she could stay for a few minutes until she could get the stuff about her history test out of her mind and feel sleepier. He put his arm around her shoulder reassuringly.

After a few more minutes, she asked if she could ask him a question. He smiled.

"How come, Daddy, childhood is so short, when it's such a wonderful time in life?"

In one brief sentence, Alice encapsulated the intensely emotional quality of saying good-bye as she readied herself to move on. Because she was a well-organized youngster, bright, insightful, expressive, perhaps even precocious, living in an orderly and caring home, she was in touch with the sadness that inevitably accompanies endings without having to blunt her feelings and pretend it wasn't there or angrily blame the world around her for her distress.

Many other youngsters are not so fortunate. Those who grow up in families in which the honest and direct expression of ideas and emotions is discouraged or simply not understood, and lack new interests in and out of school and healthy attachments to healthy contemporaries and a genuinely helpful teacher or two, usually find the experience of loss more profound and the resilience to deal with it impaired. Nor are they prepared for the series of losses that they must face during this turbulent time, such as old ambitions and infatuations that can be intense, encompassing, and so subject to whim—as when Archie Madden realized that his poor academic performance would force him to abandon his desire to be a scientist.

- ***The physical and psychological aspects of sexual maturation:***

Because the adolescent's horizons and the influences that play on him extend far beyond the confines of his family, how well or poorly he can create this new homeostasis is significantly affected by the values and standards of behavior held by his culture. With regard to sexual development, it is probably safe to assume that the majority of adolescents are much better informed about the mechanics of sex than their parents were at the same point in the life cycle. They've been exposed to sex frequently and often powerfully on television and in films. The subject is certainly more openly discussed, and the details of procreation are formally taught in many schools. In theory, removing the mystery that once surrounded sex should also reduce much of the confusion, fear, and guilt that used to accompany sexual maturation. It probably does. But, at the same time, the emerging adolescent is subject to a new set of sexual stresses as his or her curiosity is aroused, natural sexual instincts repeatedly stimulated, and the moral and ethical aspects of sex underplayed by a culture that has striven to avoid setting limits on and defining norms for sexual behavior. As the adolescent enters into this void—trying to emulate adults, but still possessed of the child's need for direction—he is extremely vulnerable to premature sexual experimentation that tends to cloud, rather than clarify, the basic challenge to learn the intimate relationship between sex, love, and family life.

The chances are that a youngster with the strengths of Alice Frohm would not be overwhelmed by these pressures, being gifted in the ability to make careful and correct distinctions in her thinking and respecting the opinions of her parents. But even such strengths are no absolute guarantee against becoming immersed in sexual confusion and failing to transit this bifurcation point successfully if some unexpected disruption were to occur in her life, such as her father's sudden death.

Cultural factors also play a powerful role. For example, I have seen numerous young men in their teens and early twenties who are haunted by a fear of homosexuality even though they are quite heterosexual in their orientation; their obsession stems in part from a sense of failure to meet the expectations of total sexual freedom and prowess the world around them seems to expect and most of their contemporaries give the appearance of enjoying. I have seen teenage girls, depressed and seriously considering suicide, whose despair can be attributed to ill-advised sexual experiences, combined with a massive denial of natural (not neurotic or socially imposed) guilt, which might otherwise have protected them against such self-defeating behavior.

Unfortunately, the best that society seems to have come up with thus far to guide adolescents through this period is an intense worship of bodily appearance, an emphasis on sexual performance as if it were the ultimate height of human accomplishment, and public warnings to use various measures other than prudence to reduce the risk of AIDS.

• *Individuation and the attainment of autonomy:*

As one grows away from one's family of origin, he must learn to be an individual, taking responsibility, understanding risk, making choices. Identifying and experimenting with talents and opportunities on the basis of which one will eventually be able to make an intelligent choice about a prospective career or occupation is an integral part of securing such autonomy.

As he learns to become independent without forfeiting the need for others, the adolescent often manifests an intense tug-of-war between his inherent and conditioned need to be dependent and his determination to be autonomous. If you've had or have teenage youngsters, you know quite well the moodiness, the times when they remind you of the little boy or girl whose company you so much enjoyed, the other times when they spend hours staring into mirrors, argumentatively refusing to go somewhere with the family on weekends because there's something much better to do with friends, answering your queries about what they want to do when school is over with a pronounced "I don't know," when you know that upstairs, in their bedrooms, are books, computer magazines, and outdoor equipment catalogues that document their most serious interests.

Privacy becomes a passion. Power struggles are often the norm, made easier in a family setting that respects individuality yet does not fail to give support and set limits, but made more difficult in a family that encourages dependence, meets defiance with defiance, assumes an exaggeratedly authoritarian stance, or presents the emerging youngster with a support system that because of indifference or misplaced tolerance, has the texture of spider-webs or quicksand.

The pursuit of autonomy involves the presence of heroes whose lives the adolescent admires and whose strengths he wishes to emulate. This situation has been made particularly difficult for many youngsters by a culture that has substituted the celebrity for the valid hero (one who, like Ulysses, has courageously overcome adversities and returns home to share his insights and wisdom with those he left behind). It has been made more difficult by events occurring within family structures that tend to destroy the positive images youngsters may once have had of their parents, that make them cynical, resentful, and self-defeating, and that pull them back from the future that should be, deservedly, theirs.

Divorce, for example. You're in your third year of college. You've just learned your parents are going to get a divorce, and your girlfriend has told you she can't continue your relationship because she wants time and space to find herself. You've been doing pretty well in your studies up until now. But as your concentration fails and you begin to feel life may be pointless, your grades fall. You had wanted to go to law school. In your dreams you had seen yourself in court, an English barrister, like the one in Alfred Hitchcock's film *The Parradine Case*—white wig, long black robe, defending an innocent, beautiful woman falsely accused of murdering her husband. You also considered you could make a pretty good living in that profession. Now you begin to worry whether you'll even win acceptance to a decent law school, and slowly your dreams fade, and you begin not to care anyway. You can't even find the energy to seek personal or career guidance. You start to worry about your parents and whether they'll be all right. Should you go home after graduation, and live with your mother to help her out, giving up your natural instinct to strike out on your own? Are you at risk for never being able to put the pieces of your life together again, drifting, aimless, searching, not finding?

- *An expansion of social relationships, involving people in authority, such as teachers and, particularly, peers:*

That the adolescent is most profoundly influenced by his contemporaries is well known. His desire for acceptance is intense, and rejection, real or imagined, can lead to serious unhappiness. Some adolescents seem to seek out marvelous relationships, while others, as if guided by some invisible magnet, seem pulled to groups that only reinforce their worst attributes. Some, by happenstance, find themselves among contemporaries who value achievement and strive to emulate them, on the football field or in the classroom; others fall prey to groups whose requirement for acceptance is the use of illicit drugs; still others, surrounded by adverse peer conditions, choose a lonely, independent track in the interest of personal survival.

"I know I wouldn't have made it without my parents being there for me," one fifteen-year-old youngster told me. "Most of the kids in school were into drugs. If you didn't use them, you were boycotted, ridiculed. The teachers looked the other way, probably because they didn't know what to do, and besides, most of the kids came from well-to-do families who pretended there wasn't any problem, and they didn't want any trouble.

"Sure, I felt unhappy . . . and tempted sometimes. But my dad had brought me up to make up my own mind about things, like everyone else in the family was encouraged to do. The basketball coach has been a big help too. Most of all, I concentrate on getting the grades to get in to a good college. In the summers, I'm a camp counselor. I've plenty of friends there. We write and sometimes see each other during the school year. It's been tough, but I'll get through it okay."

A great many contemporary stresses threaten successful transition through this critical bifurcation point in the life cycle and the creation of a healthy adolescent homeostasis. For example, the ultimate impact of the growing number of one-parent families and the epidemic occurrence of divorce has yet to be assessed. Many of these obstacles can be accounted for by an extensive dehumanization of society that experienced observers have described. More than thirty years ago, psychologist Erich Fromm predicted the "thinging" of America (not that Fromm's warnings had much effect)—such an intense focus on marketing that every individual would be seen as little more than a target to whom to sell something. Thus would vulnerable adolescents be exploited by individuals with habitually and incorrigibly criminal minds who targeted them for the sale of destructive illicit drugs. The sexual and values revolution of the late sixties and early seventies left in its wake millions of walking wounded. The great society of the eighties that was supposed to restore a spiritual sense to the culture has instead led to the pervasive preoccupation with "what's in it for me?" and the proliferation of one of the most deadly of the seven deadly sins: greed.

All in all, it's not an easy road, to say the least.

Young, Single Adulthood

Now it seems that life will go on forever. You're over twenty-one and not yet thirty, and there's more than enough time to travel, play, burn the candle at both ends . . . flounder.

For millions of young men and women, floundering seems to have become a common response at this bifurcation point, when the structure of home and school has been removed, and they have not yet built a new homeostasis as single adults. The reasons for this are not entirely clear. If their personal uncertainty and confusion is not temporarily buried by their immediately going on to graduate school with a definite goal in mind, they often, after college graduation, take jobs that hardly require the education of a bachelor's degree to perform. The more their families pressure them to take life seriously, the more they seem to postpone choices about work, about marriage, about where and how they want to begin to carve out a style of living for themselves.

The irony is that this isn't happening to youngsters who barely get through school. It's happening with some of the brightest and the best, as if they see something the adult world doesn't. Perhaps they suffer with a misplaced sense of entitlement, a disease of our age. Perhaps in the absence of sheer necessity, direction is hard to find. Or perhaps they feel the need to extend the chaos and take longer than one would expect of them to grow up, sensing that the future is indeed quite unpredictable, recognizing the dramatic acceleration of events that has occurred, and following the dictates of nature that suggested that the young, unformed, pliable creature has a better chance of evolutionary survival than the one that matures too quickly and becomes frozen, unable to adapt to drastically alien environmental conditions, in this case the upcoming twenty-first century.

Young people have not been postponing just the structuring of their work and careers. They have been looking at marriage and the starting of families in much the same way. Considering the divorce rate and the examples set by many of their parents, this does not exactly come as a surprise. Nor is it surprising that they would try to be more prepared than their predecessors to take on the responsibilities of the new homeostasis they will be constructing when they establish homes of their own. Unfortunately and inevitably, for most young people, this is a time of broken relationships, rejection, and loneliness. Nor is the search for someone with whom to share love and intimacy an easy one; the proximity of people one enjoyed within the structure of school days is gone, and the burden of creating a social network for oneself can be enormous.

Mary Rondo graduated cum laude from a small, coeducational college in Kentucky, where she had majored in English. All of her life, Mary had been a star. When she was eleven, she won an all-state contest for writing the best composition on the subject of "My Favorite Grandparent." In high school, she excelled in volleyball. Having grown up in Lexington, when it came time to go to college, she never thought of leaving the familiar surroundings that she had enjoyed so much. But when she was a junior, she began to experience a wanderlust, and developed the ambition to work in the exciting world of television.

Mary went to New York after graduating, and quickly discovered that she could not find a suitable apartment that she could afford, so she moved to a fourth-floor walk-up in nearby Jersey City, in a neighborhood that terrified her after nightfall. Making the rounds of employment agencies, she finally, in desperation, took a job as a receptionist for a network news department, hoping that by working hard, she might move into a more substantial position. However, after nearly a year, she was still answering telephones, confirming appointments, and smiling pleasantly at every person who arrived, regardless of how rudely she might be treated from time to time. Occasionally, an executive would flirt with her, suggesting that a little "give" might get her an exciting promotion; but having embraced the strict code of behavior she had been raised with, Mary rejected any and all such efforts at seduction.

Her mother wrote her often, urging her to come home. But Mary insisted that she had to find her own way, that giving up would be too much of a defeat. She did not eat well on her meager income, nor could she afford ski weekends and trips to Europe that higher up and better-paid employees at the station enjoyed. And being by nature reserved, she found it difficult to establish a group of friends. She became acquainted with one young woman who lived down the hall from her, even though the two had had little in common except youth and ambition. However, their relationship ended when Mary's neighbor invited her to a party where everyone was using cocaine and made fun of Mary because of her reluctance to do likewise.

I met Mary by sheer accident, at a party given by one of my own children. One of my daughter's friends was the daughter of friends of Mary's parents and had, as an afterthought, asked Mary to come along.

"It isn't easy," she remarked, "sticking to your standards when everyone around you is walking to a different tune. It's lonely. Besides, I'm not going anywhere with my career."

"Who is?" asked one of my daughters, who had joined the conversation. "I've been working for a year at this brokerage house, answering telephones and telling people how much they have in their money market accounts and what interest they're getting. People keep telling me it's paying dues . . . but for what? I know a couple of MBAs, one from Harvard as a matter of fact, and the work they're doing is glorified clerical work, for which they're paid a fortune."

"What do you do for a social life?" Mary asked.

"Fortunately, I grew up around here," my daughter said, "so I still have some friends around, although most of my best friends have moved away. It's not easy. My brother joined a church social group. He actually met his wife there. But that's a matter of luck."

I mentioned that a couple of patients of mine had gone on a Club Med vacation and enjoyed it greatly. And it hadn't cost them much.

"I'd be too embarrassed to do that," Mary said. "All those single people hunting for someone."

"That's not what was described to me," I said. "People of all ages, some married, some not. I guess it depends on which hotel you go to. Anyway, it's one idea, even if it's not terribly imaginative."

"What do you plan to do about your work?" Mary then asked my daughter.

"Look around. I mean, really look around. Get the names of some headhunters and sit in their waiting rooms until they see me. I guess you have to be assertive. Dad's told me it's as much a numbers game as anything else. You don't really know where the right job for you is until you knock on enough doors."

I acknowledged having given that advice. Mary was obviously thinking about what we had said.

Mary Rondo's strength was her independence and her adherence to a set of values that protected her from becoming one more victim. In the setting in which she found herself, her greatest liability was her reticence. My daughter, who saw Mary a few times after that, told me that she had sought out an assertiveness training course at one of the nearby colleges. She had quit her job and was working in a more responsible position at a public broadcasting station, planning to move to a cable network news department if and when she obtained a job there she had been interviewed for. She hadn't gone to Club Med, nor did she have a steady boyfriend, but she had become a member of the church social group to which my son had once belonged, and there she had found friends with whom she had something in common. The chances are, since she is an attractive, intelligent, and articulate young woman, Mary will eventually find someone she loves and get married, only to discover that she will face an entirely new set of stresses to deal with.

Marriage

Most of us expect the first year of marriage to be a delight. Sometimes it is. More often, it is not. For we tend to underestimate the role that the law of disruption and reintegration plays in our adjustment to giving up some of our autonomy and learning the ground rules for intimacy. This is one reason why divorce is such a common occurrence at this early stage of marriage.

Single, you feel free, unencumbered, uncommitted, unmortgaged. Then, you marry. You take on an entirely different set of self-perceptions. Instead of I, it's we. Instead of just dealing with your family, you have to deal with your partner's as well. How do you work out the particulars of everyday life, living together? You like to watch the professional football games on television in season; she (or he, as the case may be) would rather talk. One of you likes to go to antique shows on weekends; the other's more interested in getting the house decorated quickly, with standard department store furniture. One of you flares up furiously at little things and, an hour later, acts as if nothing's happened, while the other broods, feels rejected, may carry a grudge for days.

These are the years when selfishness is seriously challenged, and concentrating on doing our best to make those we live with comfortable and content requires most of us to rather radically alter the way we view things. I recall the twenty-five-year-old daughter of a good friend of mine speaking informally with me about the problems of her new marriage. She and her husband were about to celebrate their first anniversary, and she was already wondering if she should get a divorce. "Or maybe just have an affair. My husband acts as though he isn't married. We both work. After work, I go home, ready to fix dinner. But half the time he doesn't show up until eight or nine o'clock. He tells me he's just stopped by with some of the guys from work to have a drink. When I get upset, and sometimes cry, he acts as though I'm being unreasonable. I don't think we've talked about having children more than twice, and when I did bring it up, he completely ignored me. We spend every weekend with his family, every single weekend, unless I put up a fuss. But when I suggest we visit mine, he tells me to go by myself."

When I asked a few pertinent questions, I discovered that she was exaggerating the problem somewhat. Half the time with the boys was really once or twice a week. Every weekend with his family was every other, but it was true that he carried a grudge against her mother for having expressed her disapproval of the marriage for months before the wedding and was unwilling to make up with her. And he did have a very bad habit of not paying sufficient attention, not just to her suggestion about having children, but to what most people said to him.

I suggested marriage counseling. She reacted with dismay. "After only a year! I thought that was for people on the verge of divorce." I reminded her that she herself had mentioned divorce.

Some months later, I learned they had followed my advice. To her and her husband's surprise, they quickly learned new ways to promote a more intimate level of relatedness and communication, as their attention was redirected from the manifest conflicts about behavior to the underlying attitudes that had given rise to these difficulties. He began to practice listening and, making allowances for her mother's shortsightedness, to spend time with his in-laws. Both of them came to understand more clearly that giving up the old attachments to one's own family to form a new one was one of the major challenges of this time in their lives.

The Arrival of Children

Then, children come. The we is larger. Christmas photos steadily include more and more people. Who does what can become a matter of serious controversy. You are up all night and have to face another day at work, and if you are both working, who takes care of the baby? On a deeper level, who are you now? Not single. Not just married. Parents. And once you become parents, a profound (and permanent, for once a parent, always a parent) change begins to take place in how you see yourselves, touching the earliest images you have of parenting derived from your own rearing, a model you may reject or embrace or, at least, modify. What has happened to your private time? How will you still find the moment and place and motive to make love?

For me, the years when my children were small were in many ways marvelous ones, once I had recovered from the shock of becoming a parent. Like so many young men in those times, I hadn't really given too much serious thought to becoming a father. In my mid-twenties, I felt much too young for that. Holding my first child, I felt nervous, lest I drop her. I was slightly uncomfortable at being called Dad and calling my own parents Grandpa and Grandma, and couldn't help wondering at times whether my wife's attentions would turn largely from me to our new infant.

I was allowed in the delivery room for the birth of my second, and I still recall the event with a twinge of its original excitement. A few weeks later, my wife called me at the office, terrified, with the harrowing news that the baby had a hole in his heart, between one atrium and the other; to our immense relief, during the next year, the defect disappeared.

By the time our fourth child was born, I felt like a veteran; I could hardly imagine life as it had been before they came, although I was sometimes apprehensive about what it would be like when they were grown and gone. The transition was complete.

Times have since changed. Adjusting to this period in life has become far more of a challenge for millions of couples who are both working to make ends meet, and for millions of parents who are raising children by themselves, without partners at home. The fear of what may happen to ourselves takes second place to the fear of what may become of our children, a feeling that is repeatedly activated when we watch the evening news, with its graphic stories of children caught up in drug abuse and teenagers dying in unfathomable suicide pacts.

Perhaps at no other time in life is the need to give of oneself to others so vital to personal and family survival. In recent years, I have begun to see a curious sort of unhappiness pervading family life. Whether one attributes it to the narcissism of the "me" generation, to greed, or to an exclusive dedication to doing one's own thing, it clearly reflects rationalized selfishness. Bitter, miserable within themselves in spite of sometimes remarkable levels of achievement and quite comfortable living circumstances, many men and women exhibit a singular lack of concern for the well-being of others, even those they profess to love.

I recall, for example, a woman of thirty-seven, married, with two children, the manager of a very successful retail shop, who described for me her despair.

"I could have had any man I wanted when I was in my twenties. I was very attractive. I married Henry because he was the most demonstrative and persistent of my suitors . . . flowers, presents, weekends in the country. But after twelve years of living together, he just doesn't know how to please me any more. Why, would you believe, on my last birthday he had the nerve to give me luggage. Luggage! That's a really personal gift.

"I thought I wanted children. But to be honest, they've been more trouble than they're worth. Fortunately, I had a nurse when they were babies, so I could go on working. But they demand so much. I don't have the time or inclination to sit down with them and go over schoolwork. Besides, they should do it on their own. And the way they squabble . . . it makes me furious. Sometimes I want to hit them. I can't wait to send them away to boarding school.

"As for my job, I like it, but the people I work for don't appreciate how good a job I do. They don't pay me enough. They're always asking me to do more, work overtime and weekends, and then they think a little bonus at the end of the year or a party to celebrate ten years with the company is reward enough. Everyone we know has a second home except us."

When I asked her what sort of presents she gave her husband on his birthday, she couldn't recall. When I inquired as to how much she felt her children gave her by way of love and excitement, she admitted she had never thought about it that way. Nor had she given thought to the business pressures her employers had to deal with. In short, she saw the entire world strictly in terms of herself and her own largely materialistic needs and desires.

I suggested she might begin to feel better if, instead of focusing on what she felt she was not getting, she paid more attention to what she could give to her family and her coworkers. She responded to this idea with complete amazement. I tried a bit of humor, asking her what she thought of the messages in Dickens's *Christmas Carol* and Frank Capra's classic film *It's a Wonderful Life*. She hadn't read Dickens, although she had been educated at a renowned university, nor had she heard of the movie.

She was so deeply immersed in herself that she had never thought of the value of considering others and, in fact, had a slightly contemptuous attitude toward those who did. I encouraged her to take a new stance, proposing that she experiment with giving. Certainly she would not have listened to me had she not already been in pain and turned to me for solutions. Even then, it was like teaching someone a foreign language. I had to explain in clear terms tactics for giving and reward her with praise when she was considerate and thoughtful to those close to her. In the end, her efforts began to pay dividends in such obvious ways that she herself could not deny the gratification that caring about others affords.

The Single Life

Those who never marry can also find rich, fulfilling lifestyles during these years, pursuing careers, surrounded by family and friends. I recall, for example, the maiden aunt of a good friend of mine. The woman was a pediatric nurse, whose energy was dedi-

cated to the children under her care and, when she was not working, to the joys and tribulations of her parents, sisters, nephews,
nieces, and friends.

The challenge of the single life, for those who have never
married and those who are divorced or widowed, very much involves the sustenance of self-esteem and the ability to maintain a
high level of autonomy. I recall a woman of thirty-five who consulted me because she was depressed after she had ended an affair.
For nearly seven years, she had been involved with a married man
who had kept promising that one day he would leave his wife.
Wisely, she had never given up her own apartment, although he
maintained a pied-à-terre where the two of them met in the af-
ternoons, one evening a week, and on an occasional weekend.

"I was so very much in love with him," she said tearfully. "I
didn't want to face reality. I kept . . . hoping. I didn't pay any attention to the signals, like the fact he wouldn't give me his un-
listed number at home for fear I'd call him, which I would never
do, and his wife would answer the phone. I remember once when
I had to go into the hospital to have a minor procedure, he didn't
visit me. He didn't even send a card or flowers. And when his
wife finally did find out about us and gave him an ultimatum, he
just vanished. I called him once at his office. He was so rude, I
couldn't believe it was the same person."

One could have speculated that this woman had maintained
her relationship for some unconscious reason, to avoid one that
would provide her with intimacy and really work. But in her case,
that was not so. Their meeting had been quite accidental, at a sales
conference that she had attended as a marketing representative
and he as an advertising executive. He had great charm and wit,
and their sexual passion never seemed to diminish. Often she felt
guilty for being involved, a feeling that was mitigated to some extent by lurid stories of his wife's abusiveness, which she now realized had largely been lies.

Now she would have to learn to be alone again.

"If I could hate him, I might feel better," she suggested.

"If you don't feel some anger," I said, "you'd best ask yourself why. It seems to me like a pretty natural response to having been so seriously betrayed."

"How can I ever respect myself again?" she asked.

"That's a question every victim asks himself. It's a tough road back. But, except for deceiving yourself, you acted in good faith . . . although I suspect you crossed up your conscience by allowing yourself to become involved with a man who was unfaithful to his wife, whatever his given reasons."

"Conscience?" she asked. "What's that?" Her question was meant to be ironic.

"You have friends."

"Girlfriends? Plenty."

"And a good job."

"I don't know how good right now. I'm second in charge of marketing, but they're phasing out a lot of our responsibilities since the merger. I don't know what will happen to me, especially being a woman."

"You've got to be kidding . . . in this day and age?"

"You don't know the corporate world as I do," she replied. "Things are better, but discrimination is alive and well, just harder to pin down."

I saw that she had a great deal of creative work to do to survive this bifurcation point. She would have to learn to forgive herself and to live with the knowledge of her misjudgment. She would have to find a way to trust again. She would have to seriously reconsider her self-image, as a single woman and as a career woman faced with the possible threats she had described at work. She had her talents, skills, job experience, and friends to help her through this crisis, but it would call for all the independence of spirit and courage that she could find within herself.

For many of us, whether single or married, once we have adjusted to new homeostases in our lives, this stage of the life cycle can be a relatively fulfilling one. Most of us busy ourselves with the numerous details of living, so much so that we often fail to anticipate the next gigantic bifurcation point that lies directly in our path, practically around the corner: the arrival of middle age.

8

Middle Age and Beyond

Middle Age

Middle age seems to take most of us by surprise, it comes on so quickly. When you're twenty-six, you may feel you're getting terribly old. It may feel very real to you at the time, but a short while later, you can look back at twenty-six and laugh.

It's not easy to laugh about it at forty. As one friend of mine put it: "My husband and I were divorced when I was thirty-seven. I loved him a lot. But it had to happen. He was a gambler. I couldn't live with the bills and the awful uncertainty. But now, I do feel old, and strange. I spent my fortieth birthday having dinner at the Beverly Hilton hotel with a movie agent who'd been married three times, a man in his sixties whom I barely know. I kept picking at my food and wondering what I was doing there. What had happened to the person I had been? Who had I become?"

Fifty takes on even more serious dimensions. It may be a time for celebration. But it's also when you begin to count how many years have passed and how many, if you're lucky, may lie ahead.

However, the onset of middle age is a great deal more than numbers. It's a major bifurcation point, when everything is up for grabs again. Children are often grown and gone. You may have reached the pinnacle of your career, and it may not be quite what you had hoped for. With inflation, you still have money problems that refuse to go away. Perhaps you're about to be laid off because your company is trimming its fat to improve a dwindling profit picture. You know, for sure, you won't ever be pregnant again; maybe you're relieved, but when your daughter tells you she is pregnant, you may sense a touch of envy. Until now, you could usually laugh off fatigue or a slight pain in your chest or indigestion as nothing; but suddenly your health becomes a matter of very relevant concern.

I visited Janet Rice on the surgical pavilion of the New York Hospital a week after she had undergone a radical mastectomy for breast cancer. Although I was coming to see her as a friend, the head nurse on the floor, knowing of my staff affiliation, took me aside and, in a worried tone, told me she was concerned that Janet might be suicidal. Having known Janet for years, I was taken quite off guard. Apparently several of the nurses had come upon her by surprise and observed her sobbing. Janet had confided in one of them that there were times when she felt she did not want to go on living.

Indeed, when I sat with Janet myself, it was obvious to me that she was depressed. At forty-nine, she was still a very pretty woman, looking much younger than many women her age. She had made a special effort to put on a little makeup and a new dressing gown for my visit. Smiling weakly, she replied to my inquiry about how she felt. "I'm not in the best of sorts. I've never been sick a day in my life . . . really sick, I mean. Now I feel . . . mutilated."

She was worried about her husband's reaction to her illness and surgery. "Will Ed still want me sexually?" she asked. She was concerned whether she would be able to resume her usual activities, especially golf and tennis, at which she excelled. And, of course, in spite of her doctor's reassurances, she wondered if he had indeed caught the cancer in time. "What will happen to my family if I die?"

I knew, from her concerns, that she was not about to take her own life. Janet had always had a wonderful will to live and a zest for everything. She made friends easily and kept them. She had a wonderful sense of humor. Her marriage had been a solid one, and I knew Ed adored her. She had told me once: "Ed and I have had our problems, but we have a rule that when one of us is troubled by something, we talk about it and get it worked out. No going to bed on an argument. When we're wrong, we say we're sorry."

I did recall a time when, in their late thirties, Janet and Ed had had difficulties. Ed had lost his job, and they had serious financial problems. But they got through it, and I felt their marriage was stronger for having done so. And they were certainly good parents.

A quick glance around Janet's room revealed bouquet after bouquet of flowers, from numerous friends including myself. On the table next to her bed sat a picture of Ed and their two children looking very grown up.

"I know my limitations," she told me. "I'm not very creative." I silently disagreed. "I don't like uncertainty." Most people don't, I thought. "That makes this business especially upsetting for me. No matter what the doctor says, I know that no one can be sure of the outcome. I don't go to church as much as I probably ought to . . . but I still believe."

Toward the end of our visit, Ed arrived, carrying mail. He walked straight to Janet and kissed her, before turning to me and shaking my hand firmly. Janet teased him: "They decided I needed a psychiatrist," she said. Ed and I laughed. I thought of the nurse's comments to me earlier, spoken with the best of intentions, and of how so many doctors and nurses didn't seem to know what to do when their patients cried or showed any evidence of falling apart in the face of even the most threatening of stressful situations.

The stresses of entering middle age can be enormous. It is a time to reorient oneself to one's work, sometimes to accept the fact that this is as far as you will ever come, sometimes to ac-

knowledge that your skill to earn your living has been made obsolete by technological progress, sometimes to deal with the many
and varied problems associated with unique success. This is when
you have more or less lost control over your children's futures.
You've done all that you could do, and now they're on their own;
but, as parenting never ends, you have to struggle with the natural
tendency to live their lives for them, if only in your imagination,
and once more go through the anguish of confusion and loneliness you may well have known when you were their age yourself.

How well prepared you will be to do this—in fact, how well
you will meet any and all challenges of this bifurcation point and
of the homeostatic stage of life it leads to—will be determined by
how well you have transited the earlier stages of your own life
cycle.

"My wife's never been able to face the fact that the children
are gone," Jeff O'Brien told me, sitting on the terrace of the Bux-
ton Point hotel, overlooking the Maine coast. I'd known Jeff casu-
ally over the years, but this vacation was the first time I'd seen him
every day for two straight weeks, and he had become increasingly
intimate in his personal disclosures.

"In fact," he went on, "you could say we're both depressed
for different reasons. I was glad to see the kids go. Miriam just
gloomed around. She put off seeing people. She had a rough time
with her change of life. Sometimes, at night, she'd sit within a few
feet of the phone all evening hoping she'd hear from one of
them . . . the kids, I mean.

"Here I was, at the top, chairman of the board. Sure, it's a
small company, but I own most of it. I've even got an offer to sell
out. But what would I do if I did? That's depressing."

Miriam was a fairly attractive woman, I thought. Jeff had
everything. Even their children were in pretty good shape, a married daughter with two children and a son in medical school. On
the surface, he seemed to have little to complain about.

It was two in the afternoon. Jeff ordered his third vodka
martini. As he spoke, I discovered more of the answers to his
discontent.

Being a mother had been Miriam's sole ambition. After she married Jeff, she insisted that they live a short distance from her own family so she could continue the close relationship she had with her mother. It seemed reasonable enough at the time. As the years went by, Jeff began to suspect that Miriam had married him because he was the best prospect around, and while they seemed to be compatible, he never really felt that she loved him as he thought she should or as he felt he loved her.

"That sort of gave Miriam the upper hand, you know," he said. "'He who loves most, hurts most,' the saying goes, or something like that. My God, she fussed over those kids. When they went off to college, you'd think the world had ended. She wanted to visit every other weekend, and only when our daughter had a heart-to-heart talk with her did she come to her senses. I love the kids, but I almost came to hate them in a crazy way."

Jeff had been to engineering school. He had invented some manufacturing process that I did not understand, and with the patents had built a substantial business.

"Now I feel burned out," he said. "I'm bored by the business, but if I sell it, I don't know what I'd do with myself. I never had any other interests. You couldn't even call me an inventor. I never did invent anything else."

He put his fingers to the dark shadows underneath his eyes.

"What do you think?" he asked. "Think I look my age? When I was in college, people used to say I resembled Tyrone Power. You're a doctor. How safe is . . . plastic surgery?"

It was obvious to me that Jeff and Miriam had reached middle age with many assets, ranging from financial security to the successful life adjustment of their children and their own physical well-being. I knew so many couples whose middle years were replete with serious problems that I felt that these two should really be thankful for their fate. But at the same time, I could see how they had come to this impasse. Miriam had never understood what it was to separate herself from her own family; dependent, she unwittingly wanted to raise her own children to go on needing her indefinitely, a task at which she had, fortunately, failed. Jeff had had a brief period of inventiveness early in his life, had capitalized on it, but had never nurtured this talent nor taken an interest in anything other than his business that might serve him to reshape his life when the primary thrust of work had run its course.

The past is indeed prologue. The two of them had a lot of work to do if they were to pass through this bifurcation point and adjust to this life stage successfully. As we barely knew each other, Jeff didn't impress me with his insightfulness, and our relationship was not a professional one, I felt it best to finesse the responsibility.

"Have you thought of taking up golf?" I asked.

Middle age is a time when marriages again must themselves go through an episode of disruption and reintegration to be revitalized. Issues of intimacy, communication, shared interests, and mutual respect come again to the fore, and if these cannot be successfully resolved, one may well face another serious stress common to this time in life, divorce, the incidence of which rises sharply during this vulnerable period.

New identities. More "interesting times," full of risk, fear, loneliness, the unpredictable. "I don't think I've ever been so terrified in my life," Irene Webb recounted, "as when I walked out of that lawyer's office and tried to find my way to the subway uptown. I felt utterly confused. I stood on the corner of Broad and Wall for ten minutes, in the bitter cold, not knowing which way to go. Finally, I asked a messenger boy, who looked at me like I was crazy and pointed me to the IRT station at Broadway. When I got back home, I lay down on the bed and sobbed like a five-year-old."

I'd been to college with Irene's husband, Charlie. I'd been an usher in their wedding. Irene was not a pretty girl, but in her bridal finery, she'd assumed a tall, stately radiance, smiling, her red hair tucked neatly in a bun. It had made me think that she was the kind of woman who would probably age rather gracefully. She had.

I still don't know for sure what went wrong between them that led, thirty-two years and three children later, to threaten the end of their life together. Charlie had done well financially; he owned a foreign car dealership in New Jersey. They lived in Manhattan, at his request—he liked the excitement of it—and he maintained he did not mind the reverse commute each day. Their children were in private schools and, as far as I knew, all right. I didn't see them more than once every few years. I hadn't seen Irene in over a year when she phoned to tell me about the divorce and ask if we could talk.

"Charles had an affair," she admitted with considerable embarrassment. "His secretary. We're going to be fifty-five next year, and he runs off with a twenty-seven-year-old . . . I won't use the word . . . who probably manicures her toenails while she's watching television quiz shows." She struggled to contain her rage.

"Maybe he's going through some kind of breakdown," I said.

"I know that. He's been impossible for nearly a year, yelling, abusive to me, staying out all hours of the night, disappearing weekends, leaving all kinds of traces of what he's been up to around the apartment."

"Have you tried counseling?"

"You don't understand. Charles intends to marry her."

I was surprised.

"I offered to go to a marriage counselor, but Charles refused. I asked my attorney to ask him if he'd consider a reconciliation. He told me I was out of my mind . . . advised me to cooperate with the divorce and get it over with. He even suggested I might want to get married again someday and I'd be better off to be free of entanglements in case, for some wild reason, he changed his mind."

I asked how their children were taking things. They were, as I expected, silently in pain.

"I can't sleep. I've lost fifteen pounds. I feel so alone. I don't know what I'm going to do without him."

Irene hadn't asked to talk with me because I was a psychiatrist, although that may not have been entirely irrelevant. I was, as it turned out, the only person she felt she could confide in, and because I was someone who had known Charlie over the years, she hoped I might be able to give her some insight into what had happened.

"In one way, Irene," I said, "it doesn't make any sense. But in another, it sounds as though he's trying to relive his adolescence or make up for lost time somehow. Charlie didn't date much, you know."

"We were like . . . childhood sweethearts. That's all the more reason I can't understand."

"He was a pretty vain guy, Irene. Charlie would hate the idea of getting old. But, by itself, that couldn't explain it. I think the fact that he was never very introspective . . . Charlie's never dealt in feelings. As a matter of fact, I wondered sometimes how anyone could ever develop the kind of intimacy with Charlie that could make a marriage, or even a friendship, meaningful."

"You're not just saying that to make me feel I haven't lost as much as I feel I've lost," she said.

"No. But it's a question you should ask yourself. Right now, you're feeling terribly rejected, for a younger woman, obviously. That's a hurt you're going to have to get over. I think that if you can see that the relationship you and Charlie had involved the mechanics of marriage more than its soul, it may make things easier for you to accept . . . and free you to do what you have to, build a new life for yourself, Irene."

"I always let Charles have his own way. I let myself get swallowed up. You could say I asked for this. But then, I suppose, if I'd stood my ground, maybe the marriage would have ended sooner. Charles didn't like people to disagree with him about anything."

I knew, of course, that had Irene held on to her own identity with greater determination, there was a chance that Charlie might have respected her more and made a few adjustments of his own. Or he might have walked out sooner. That was a risk she probably should have taken. Had their relationship undergone smaller crises, more contained episodes of disruption leading to new, more viable homeostases over the years, it might not have ended with such a bang and, in fact, might well not have ended at all.

Now Irene would have to sort things out. She could begin with her children, staying close to them. She could spend more time with her friends. She could even start dating, and perhaps find a love to replace the one she'd lost—and this time know better what to look for and how to handle it. She would have to release herself from her hurt and anger, lest it turn into a lasting resentment that would only eat away at her.

Ironically, Irene would even have to prepare herself for the possibility that a somewhat penitent and chagrined Charlie might come home, plead for forgiveness, and ask to try again. This is exactly what did happen, three weeks before they were to sign the final separation papers. Irene informed him that she could take the chance only if their marriage assumed a new level of closeness and sharing. Charlie agreed.

"If humiliation is good for the soul," Charlie later told me privately, "my soul must be in very good shape. I can't even take credit for the outcome. The bimbo had another boyfriend, some stallion lifeguard down on the Jersey beach she was seeing at the same time she was telling me what a wonderful life we were going to have together. When it was all over, I felt so . . . old, and tired. Thank God, Irene had the generosity to take me back."

That was five years ago, only yesterday. And now that I think of it, Charlie and Irene are getting ready for the next major bifurcation point in their life cycle: their sixtieth birthdays.

Aging

My family, including my children, softened the blow of sixty by giving not one but three separate birthday dinners for the occasion. There were some rewards to getting on, I thought; after all the years of picking up the tab, this time it wasn't on me. I felt wealthy in their friendship and love. It was good to celebrate. It was good to dream and talk of all the things I wanted to do, even if the sense of having less time than one might want to do them all in echoed in the back of my mind.

They say that in the last moments of life, your past flashes before your eyes, a rush of vivid memories. Well, it happens a lot sooner, about now, and, I suspect, continues indefinitely. Things like snowstorms, and picnics, and graduations, and even funerals. Funerals come to mind because now you begin to notice that a number of people you've known for years are dying, in clusters, as if the earth, turning, is shedding some of its excess baggage to make room for what is to come. Alfred, Lord Tennyson, described this experience in his poem "Ulysses": "Though much is taken, much abides."

I had occasion recently to see a patient in consultation, a woman in her mid-eighties suffering with severe, painful arthritis and reported depression. I went to her home, where the maid showed me into the bedroom. She was propped up against large, silk pillows, waiting for my visit. I was supposed to be there to solve one of her major problems, insomnia, and would do so with tiny doses of a commonly used antidepressant drug.

For the problem of getting older, of course, I had no easy remedy. Having already observed that she had a keen sense of humor, I answered her question as to what else I might do for her by saying, with a smile, I would help her get more out of life's "golden years."

"Golden years!" she exclaimed, throwing her arms up in a wild gesture that was meant to be amusing. "Golden years!" she repeated. "Let me tell you. The golden years are made of some kind of lousy alloy. But if you have a reasonable amount of good health, I suppose they beat the alternative."

Retirement

The death rate among retirees during the first year after retirement is remarkably high; this statistic must be attributed in part to being unprepared for the disruption that normally accompanies this transition, the loss of work that gave meaning and identity to one's life. My own father set an invaluable example of how to grow old by never really retiring. On paper, he seemed to have retired when he resigned his position as head of a small business enterprise. But he was ready to pick up the pieces of his new life and fulfill dreams he had entertained for years but never had had the time to go after. He sold our home and built a new one on waterfront property on the Shrewsbury River in New Jersey, on an acre he had purchased at the bottom of the Depression. Nearly seventy, he bought a powerboat, which he had always wanted but had been too busy to acquire, learned how to master it, and sailed great distances for years. Finally, as he was approaching eighty, early one summer morning, on the beach where he had gone to watch the gulls—another of his many interests—he slumped to the sand and died. I remember him saying to me, only a few months before his death: "I've had this thought that keeps coming into my head, sort of nostalgic, something I recall from a long time ago, about streetlights going on and it being time to go home."

Amy Lewis was a woman in her early seventies when I met her, a thin, slightly built, elegant person, soft-spoken and intelligent. She had become quite anxious about what she perceived to be a growing tendency toward forgetfulness.

"I walk out of the house and forget to lock the doors. I leave the keys in my car when I park it at the grocery. I can look for hours to find my checkbook. I always had a superb memory. I don't know what's happened. It scares me."

I reassured her, as soon as I was sure, that she was not suffering with what she dreaded most, Alzheimer's disease. She was simply preoccupied, and under tension, which only exaggerated the natural diminution in active memory that does occur as one gets older.

Amy had lost her husband a year earlier. She'd been married to Andrew for nearly fifty years. They had no living children; a daughter had died of pneumonia at three. Although she had tried, she had not been able to become pregnant again; they decided against adoption. Andrew had been a social caseworker. She herself had opened a small neighborhood retail shop where she prepared baskets of delicacies for customers to order as gifts on birthdays, holidays, or whenever the impulse came upon them.

"Andrew and I hardly ever argued," Amy said. "That doesn't mean we always got on and didn't disagree. But we shared so many of the same interests and values, and we loved each other. Andrew looked after the things I have to do now all by myself, taxes, driving the car, dealing with the landlord at my store."

Amy had grown up in a small Ohio town near the West Virginia border. Her parents had encouraged all their children to be independent. When she graduated from high school, while most of her classmates went to work, her parents sent Amy off to college in New England. Following her graduation, she worked for a furniture design house in Boston for several years. After she met and married Andrew, they bought the house in Salem they lived in the rest of their lives.

Amy was well known in town and noted for her spirit and energy. She was active in politics. She fought for historic preservation. She was always there to give a helping hand to friends in time of trouble.

"Even though we lived in Salem," she said smiling, "I never did come to believe in witches."

She had been shattered when her daughter died. But Andrew was there for her and she for him. Her sister came in from Chicago on an overnight train and stayed with her for a month.

"I'm starting to outlive everyone," she said. "What if this memory problem gets worse? What if I end up totally helpless?"

Before she came to see me, her family physician had given her small doses of an antidepressant. "He was a new doctor. He didn't really know me. He didn't have much time to talk." A friend of Amy's from Boston suggested she take the shuttle to New York and have at least one visit with me.

"Grief can do this," I told her. She knew that already. I also complimented her on her openness to reaching out for help when she needed it and doing so without embarrassment. "All my life I've helped people," she said. "You shouldn't give if you don't know how to receive too."

Altogether, Amy and I spent two hours together. She felt better for having talked about things and for knowing that even though she might never see me again and we were hundreds of miles apart, she could call me if she wanted. She'll be eighty-three this year. A few weeks ago she telephoned to see if I was all right. I assured her I was.

How can we increase the chances of coping well with the challenges of aging? Recalling that each stage in the life cycle builds on the ones that have preceded it, now, in the final phase, we pay the price or reap the rewards of what we have sown. If we have learned to adapt to changing circumstances, we will adapt to these. If we know how gracefully, though not without grief, to let go of what we can no longer hold on to—health, loved ones, friendships, careers—we will be less prone to thrash against the inevitability of loss. If we have cultivated independence, we shall keep going as long as we are able, and if we have allowed ourselves to need, we can accept the help that others, whom we have given to over the years, can now give to us. Social security and retirement pension plans help too.

So does creativity. Human imagination has been described as the most lasting organizer of experience and, at the same time, the most durable organizer of new structures in the present. As we grow older, we can take encouragement from the example of creative genius and, on a more modest scale, of course, use our own creativity as part of our coping armamentarium. It is remarkable how often creative individuals in a wide variety of fields—physics, architecture, medical science, painting, sculpting—show a late-life increment in the rate of production of outstanding works. Benjamin Franklin was seventy-eight when he invented bifocal glasses. William Carlos Williams published three volumes of verse between the time he suffered a stroke, at sixty-eight years of age, and his death at seventy-nine. Leopold Stokowski was conducting in the recording studio in his mid-nineties, and Alfred Hitchcock was making films well into his seventies. What is remarkable about such works is the way in which they sum up the creator's life endeavor and reflect the strength and endurance of his imagination.

When we're infants or children, we have more internal plasticity than we will have at any time in our lives. Because we're so flexible then, it is crucial to be surrounded by constant, predictable, supportive structures in our environment. We are utterly dependent, deriving much of our identity from the way in which others look at us. As we grow up, we become more independent, coming to rely more and more on ourselves for self-esteem. We still need others, of course, but in ways that involve more give-and-take, and sometimes more give than take. Our competence—in work, in human relationships, in the details of daily living, in overcoming adversity and meeting challenge, in reaching for our dreams—grows. If we enjoy an average degree of good fortune, our physical health and stamina endure. However, as we pass into our sixties and seventies, we gradually become more dependent again. How others value us makes even more of a difference than it seemed to only a few years before. We hold on to some skills and lose others. We begin to descend from a peak of personal adult adaptability and freedom, and for a different—but no less relevant—set of reasons, like a child once more, we need familiar and sustaining structures around us to make us feel secure, wanted, worthwhile.

Of course, old age will be easier for those of us who have practiced resilience throughout our lives than for those who have not, even as it will be easier for those who have practiced love. It would be a mistake for us to count on three ghosts arriving in our bedrooms on Christmas Eve, as happened to old Scrooge, to offer us metamorphosis and the chance for last-minute salvation.

9

A Not-So-Small Matter of Unfinished Business

NO ONE emerges from one phase of the life cycle into a new homeostatic structure with all the business of personal growth completed. There are always unsettled matters of greater or lesser import that remain to cause problems and that require further resolution.

In general, the earlier in life that failures to cope with the demands of adaptation occur, the more serious the consequences. Consider childhood. During childhood, everything is at stake, for here, the fundamental pillars of personality are being formed for the first time. Hence, self-image and self-esteem, a growing sense of competence and autonomy, the ability to form human relationships, and resilience itself are taking shape. Any disruption in a child's health and the consistent and supportive environment that he needs to master this process—the death of a parent, abuse, rejection, abandonment, an atmosphere of fear or hostility—will skew or seriously impede these events. The consequences can be felt throughout a lifetime, when bifurcation points and the inevitable disruption that accompanies them appear.

For example, the overly dependent child will face greater

hardships when he or she arrives at adolescence and is confronted by the imperative to move away from home to engage a larger world. On the other hand, the child who, because of parental neglect or cruelty, has had to learn early on to be excessively independent, shut out his or her feelings, and renounce the natural helplessness that is part of childhood may well find himself unable to depend on others, trust them, and form intimate human relationships throughout his lifetime.

It is during childhood that one's strengths and limitations in mastering the rest of life are most significantly defined. They will persist, for good or ill, unless, during some future episode of disruption, the person becomes aware of the need to change or is literally forced by circumstances and inner pain to do so.

At the bifurcation point that introduces adolescence, everything is at risk. No longer can one turn primarily to others to find self-respect; the search is internalized as well. For the first time, external conditions of life begin to change radically, in no small measure because the youngster's power over his environment increases and he is, at the same time, ever more vulnerable to influences beyond the confines of his family. For the first time, he faces the real stress of letting go of people and things to which he has become attached; with his growing capacity to look within himself for insights, he will become familiar with what it is to feel hours, or even days, of melancholy; all other things being equal, his moods will be balanced by his youthful enthusiasm and naive anticipation of the future.

Certain challenges take precedence as the adolescent seeks greater independence, explores his imagination and the opportunities of the real world to determine what course his future work may take, experiments with human relationships to discover their richness and their limitations. Like the child, he is still in a profoundly formative stage of life. Failure here, because of lingering, unresolved issues carried over from childhood or adverse conditions at the time, can carry with it repercussions that may reduce his ability to deal with the bifurcation points that still lie ahead.

For example, should he fail to learn what his talents are, or should he be denied the chance to cultivate them, his career choices may be seriously limited—even quite wrong—and, during the subsequent years of adulthood, he may well search in vain for the self-esteem and fulfillment that one derives from work well done. Should he fail to learn the intricacies of human relationships, he risks turning out to be a poor marital partner or parent.

Future bifurcation points may offer the adolescent the chance to learn what he does not learn at this point in time, whether these points occur naturally or are induced by unexpected, profoundly stressful events.

From the onset of young adulthood and carrying through to middle age, one is subject to what might well be viewed as variations on a theme. The pattern that each life takes assumes greater and greater individuality. Such universal issues as maintaining and recovering self-respect and balancing independence against one's need for others continue, although the degree to which one or another particular challenge enters into each life will depend on the character and shape of that life. For example, one person, unmarried at thirty-seven, may have to make an extra effort to build a network of meaningful human relationships, as there's no one automatically in place, such as children; another, also thirty-seven but married, may have to practice the skills of reconciliation and the art of intimacy in order to strengthen the nature of family bonds; a third, suddenly widowed at a young age, may be thrust into a lifestyle that demands considerably more autonomy than he or she has ever had to generate before.

The summation of all that we have built over the years—within ourselves and in the world around us—determines how well prepared we shall be when we come face-to-face with middle age and beyond. Will we be surrounded by and part of a stimulating, caring, and supportive family, or will we find ourselves awash in conflict and hostility, or isolated and alone? Will we be involved in meaningful, rewarding work, or overwhelmed with financial pressures, office politics, disenchantment, boredom, or even chronic unemployment? Will we know how to adapt to changing circumstances, which often dominate this period in life, or will we find ourselves especially hampered because we have learned neither to cope with loss nor to restore self-esteem when the sources of it to which we have become accustomed, such as youthfulness or the acclaim of others, begin to fade? Will we have preserved sufficient inner resources so that falling apart as we enter middle age can be an opportunity to make up for past failures and engage in significant reconstruction of our lives and personalities?

Martha Devoe is an example of a woman who, because she had not satisfactorily transited several earlier bifurcation points in her life cycle, arrived at middle age quite unprepared. When she did, she fell apart, but was able to use her experience with disruption to reshape herself and her life.

Martha had not been as fortunate as Alice Frohm. Childhood had not been easy for her. She had no father with whom to share special moments and inner feelings. Instead, an alcoholic, he was often physically abusive to her and her mother, and instilled only fear. As a result, Martha became an expert at running away.

First, she ran away to school, where she did adequately in her studies and surrounded herself with a number of good girlfriends. Then, at nineteen, she ran away from home to marry her high school boyfriend.

"I was young, headstrong. I wanted to be on my own. My parents would never have let me marry Bob if I'd asked them. What a fool I was. Three years after we married, I had a one-year-old baby and was living in a trailer camp, and Bob had run off with some frump who worked at the local drugstore. I was terribly unhappy, and scared too. I thought of doing myself in, but I had the baby. So I did the only thing I could think of doing. I ran home.

"I stayed there for five long, lousy years, listening to Dad scream at Mom and Mom crying in the bathroom and telling me to get away when I knocked on the door to ask her if she was all right. Finally, I couldn't stand it any more. I moved to Teaneck, New Jersey, only a few miles from my parents' house in Englewood, but a million light-years away as far as I was concerned. I got a job as a secretary once Bobby junior started school, and checked into night school at the community college. I got my degree, but not for another ten years. I met Ralph there. He was divorced. He seemed to like little Bobby. I was lonely. So, like a dummy, I married him. I thought that because he had joined AA, he had overcome his problem with booze. He stayed sober for six weeks! We got a civil annulment, and I never saw or heard from him again.

"Then I met Harrison. I thought he was everything I'd dreamed of. I didn't know he was married at first. He didn't tell me that until we'd decided to get married ourselves. We had to wait another year and a half for his divorce to be final. But I was head over heels in love with him. And he had money. We could live in a nice house. I could hold my head up again, being married to an accountant."

I met Martha when she was forty-one, decades after she had failed to successfully weather the special challenges of her teenage and young adult years. My wife had known her from a tennis group she played with from time to time, and had asked me if I would mind if she brought Martha over for coffee some Saturday morning to see if I could help her, or at least persuade her to seek some kind of counseling. With ordinary reluctance, I agreed.

Martha told me her story. "The last six years have been a nightmare. I can't live with Harrison and I can't live without him. He's a devil. One minute he's hitting me, the next he's bringing me flowers and wanting to make love. I've tried to leave, but I can't. I'm afraid to. Where would I go? What would I do? He'd kill me, I know, or get a tough lawyer and see that I wouldn't get a dime to live on."

She kept swirling the spoon in her coffee nervously, until she spilled some on the table. Her hands were trembling.

"I don't know what to do. Bobby's in college. My father's dead. Mom's in a nursing home."

Suddenly, she pulled up the sleeve of her blouse, revealing dark black-and-blue bruises, freshly made. In her eyes I thought I caught the look of innocent naïveté of the small child she had once been.

I had certainly known other Marthas, caught in the framework of a disturbed family growing up, the kind of conflict-laden household that is ironically much harder to leave than a home that is stable, loving, open, and nurturing, when, in adolescence, the time for leaving comes. Instead of learning how to be herself and gradually separate from her parents, the only exit Martha could figure out was to escape by impulsively marrying Bobby. Then, instead of using her freedom after that marriage broke up to find herself and complete the job of adolescence by discovering some measure of autonomy, she rushed home to her parents again.

When she finally mustered the strength to leave once more and had started to create a life of her own, Martha's special limitations—dependence, vulnerability to loneliness, lack of self-esteem—propelled her into her brief marriage with Ralph, which proved to be only another disaster. Although utterly demoralized by this mistake, she learned nothing from the experience, attributing her misfortune largely to bad luck and blaming Ralph entirely for what had gone wrong. Had her perception of reality been sufficiently disrupted at that time so that she could have looked into herself for solutions, as painful, humbling, and bewildering as that might have been for her, she might have made use of this opportunity for change. But she did not.

Thus, when Harrison arrived on the scene, wishful thinking took precedence. She ignored the obvious warning signs of his cruelty—sarcasm, for example, and intentional insensitivity to her feelings—and fled into the relationship with him like an infatuated youngster. Once caught in this, her third marriage, she was frightened to leave, remaining in a highly abusive and confusing collaboration that seemed destined to make her more helpless and victimized than she had ever been in her life.

Now, however, the cumulative stresses of his behavior, her grief for her father, having to place her mother in a nursing home, and her son's being away at college seemed finally to have exerted sufficient pressure on her system to disrupt her previously inflexible personality structure so that perhaps, at last, she could face the un-finished business of her youth and learn to meet life head-on.

I could not help asking myself how Martha Devoe had en-dured so much for so long. Ironically, I thought, in spite of all she had been through, she did show some evidence of resilience. From time to time, she had shown bursts of independence, how-ever short-lived. She had a high tolerance for frustration and conflict (which had been learned early in life and did not always serve her well). She possessed a sense of humor. She had not stopped praying. What she obviously lacked was meaningful in-sight into herself and a consistent autonomy that would enable her to tolerate an unstructured world around her, with the pain of loneliness, long enough to gain the command she required to find her place in life and relationships that would support her in her need to grow.

I did what I was expected to do and what seemed appropriate. I suggested she consult an attorney and consider counseling with a professional. What she needed at this point in her life was an an-chor to windward, someone she could trust and rely on to give her enough support and some measure of insight to permit her to escape (once more) the malevolent structure in which she now found herself, but to do so while gaining the autonomy she should have developed in her teenage years and, with it, a greater sense of self.

Although I never saw Martha again, I heard she followed my advice. It wasn't easy to extricate herself legally from Harrison. But she did. She apparently found a job as secretary to a corporate executive in Morristown. She renewed some of her old friend-ships that she had let slide over the years. She seemed to have put aside her desperate search for love and marriage, learning to live comfortably alone. As a matter of fact, she did marry again, ten years later, at age fifty, and according to my sources, that marriage has worked out well. Consequently, she should be much better able to face the challenges of aging, when once again self-esteem is on the line, the external circumstances of life steadily change, and, as in adolescence, loss becomes an everyday concern.

Martha Devoe's story exemplifies the strong interdependency that each phase of the life cycle has in relationship with those that went before and those that lie ahead. While certain common issues recur in each stage of life and are challenged at each bifurcation point, these will obviously not appear with the same intensity or assume equal importance in everyone's life. Some of us will struggle forever to cope with too much dependence. Others will have to make a special effort to give and to forgive. Still others will carry an excess of sensitivity and a fragile sense of self-esteem, for which we will repeatedly have to compensate by questioning the accuracy of feelings of hurt and rejection and reminding ourselves that we are, in fact, leading worthwhile lives.

Each bifurcation point represents a new opportunity to strengthen ourselves, if we possess sufficient resilience. Avoiding this challenge only serves to postpone the learning that we are meant to accomplish at that time and weaken us in our ability to face future stresses. Ignoring or sidestepping this mandate carries with it the promise that the tensions produced by unresolved conflicts and the perpetuation of faulty coping behavior will mount, until one day, in the end, we shall be forced to pay the price for our failure, not infrequently in an experience of dramatic disruption, at times a veritable explosion, that many doctors still mistakenly refer to as illness. Even under such circumstances, the resilience we have will stand us in good stead, and the chaos we experience can offer us an invaluable chance to develop more.

PART III

The Resilient Personality

1 0

The Resilient Personality

F R O M Y E A R S of observation of people like those I've already described—some friends, some patients, some seen from afar—I have been able to assemble a profile of the resilient personality. My more resilient patients, many of whom I consider healthier in many ways than millions who have never had the insight or motivation to reach out for guidance, knew they were in trouble and sought help from someone. That the someone happened to be a psychiatrist may have been partly a coincidence of our times, as psychiatrists and other mental health professionals have come to fill a void in a society that has disrupted the nuclear and extended family, encouraged individual isolation and distrust, and professionalized practically every aspect of living. These people were motivated to make things better, if only because of the pain they found themselves unable to tolerate or escape. They were in search of solutions. The more resilient they were, the more quickly they were able to form a trusting, collaborative relationship with me, their therapist, one that was appropriately dependent (because I was an authority figure, to whom they had turned for relief and insight), yet without fear that they would have to forfeit their own sense of basic autonomy in the process. They learned rapidly. They often were able to identify the more obvious life situations or inner conflicts that had brought them to a point of crisis.

As therapy proceeded and I pointed out things to them that they might not have considered before, they were able to give up distorted or obsolete ways of looking at important issues and to integrate new perspectives and patterns of behavior into their approach to coping. They reacted emotionally, weeping, expressing anger, sharing their fears and hopes; they could regain control of their feelings as they moved on to other topics or when our time together had come to an end. And when our work together was completed (at least the more formal aspects of therapy, as unlearning and relearning is a lifelong process), they could terminate their regular visits without undue distress—in fact, with the optimistic conviction that they could take command of their lives quite well.

I discovered more about the nature of the resilient personality from patients and friends who had survived combat experience and prisoner of war internment. One had served with the army in China during the Second World War. Another had landed with the commandos just before the major troop landing at Normandy on D-Day. Two of my close friends had spent four years in Japanese prisoner of war camps. Their experiences, plus the extensive scientific literature about survival that I have already discussed, gave me important additional insights into the matter.

A third source of data was my investigation of the nature of the creative process. Behavioral scientists who have been studying creativity for several decades have drawn conclusions about the process and about the attributes of the creative personality that are particularly relevant to resilience. For example, employing standardized psychological tests to identify personality traits commonly associated with a high degree of skill at creative problem solving, they have shown that people who perform very well at looking at old problems in new ways, coming up with new options and choosing the more suitable and workable solutions to various dilemmas, also seem best able to deal with challenge and sustain or restore personal coherence under stressful conditions.

The more creative a person is, the more likely he is to be independent in thought and action; possess a strong, but supple, sense of self-esteem; be receptive to new ideas; exhibit a wide range of interests; tolerate uncertainty and distress for a prolonged, though reasonable, length of time; enjoy mystery as much as definitiveness; and commit himself to life, his work, and the people with whom he is involved within the framework of a meaningful philosophy of life.

What emerged from these various sources was a set of resilient attributes that, when I put them together, came as no real surprise to me. These include the following:

- A strong, supple sense of self-esteem
- Independence of thought and action, without fear of relying on others or reluctance to do so
- The ability to give and take in one's interactions with others, and a well-established network of personal friends, including one or more who serve as confidants
- A high level of personal discipline and a sense of responsibility
- Recognition and development of one's special gifts and talents
- Open-mindedness and receptivity to new ideas
- A willingness to dream
- A wide range of interests
- A keen sense of humor
- Insight into one's own feelings and those of others, and the ability to communicate these in an appropriate manner
- A high tolerance of distress
- Focus, a commitment to life, and a philosophical framework within which personal experiences can be interpreted with meaning and hope, even at life's seemingly most hopeless moments

The caveat for any such list of wonderful traits is, of course, that none of us is perfect. We are always more or less any one of these things: a little weak on self-esteem, perhaps, but quite open to new ideas; enjoying a wide range of interests, but having trouble focusing on one or two to develop more fully; gifted with a sense of humor, but so tolerant of distress that we put up with unhealthy, demeaning, even abusive behavior in others for much too long a time; willing to dream of what we wish to accomplish with our lives, but finding it hard to muster up the self-discipline required to take the often arduous steps involved.

Periods of stress frequently represent unique opportunities to develop or strengthen those resilience qualities that are not our strongest suits. I recall a twenty-seven-year-old man, the son of a very close friend of mine, whom I had known since childhood, whose movement into young adulthood was being impeded by unfinished business carried over from adolescence. He certainly possessed many aspects of resilience. He was a marvelous wit; he could quickly mimic any number of celebrities, and his amusing comments were guaranteed to make me laugh whenever we spent time together. He was warm, made friends easily, always thought of others. Optimistic, open-minded, and reasonably well organized, he performed well as a very junior executive in an insurance company, the first job he had obtained after college graduation.

But, somehow, he could not put it all together. He was visibly unhappy. He wanted desperately to be a genuine entrepreneur, working on his own. He had plenty of ideas, any one of which he might have tried to implement; but he was afraid to take the risks—of being without the structure of employment, of having to sustain the long, intense discipline required to succeed, of the humiliation if he failed, of the unknown. Consequently, he had great difficulty maintaining his self-respect. Although he could afford his own apartment, he still lived at home with his parents and unmarried younger sister.

From the time he began dating more seriously, when he was seventeen, he tended to become quickly involved emotionally with each particular girl. Although he was persistently indecisive about getting married, at first because of his youth, but later on without any specific reason, he would go to any lengths to preserve a relationship, until the young woman, frustrated by his inability to make a commitment, would break it up. He would then go through a short, but intense, period of grief, but, being charming and sociable, he had little trouble finding a new girlfriend with whom to engage in a similar sort of liaison.

It was obvious to me that in spite of his many talents, this young man was handicapped by an obscure but pervasive sense of helplessness, which in turn fostered his dependence. Because I was familiar with his family, I knew to some extent how this state of affairs had come about. Both parents had grown up during the Depression and both had suffered serious financial hardship, a condition they were determined their own children would not have to experience if they could prevent it. His father's father had been a grocery store manager, a harsh, driving man, who relentlessly pushed his sons (but, consistent with his scheme of values, not his daughters) to achieve from the minute they began school. My friend became an accountant. He and his wife focused almost exclusively on making their own children happy and avoided bringing any pressure whatsoever on them. Yet, ambition and the spirit of independence were subtly, and sometimes not so subtly, undermined for years. For example, when it came time for the young man to apply to college, he was advised by several of his teachers to attend practice SAT courses to help improve his scores and his chances for acceptance at a good university; his parents scoffed at the idea. And when, after he had earned his bachelor's degree, he expressed an interest in graduate school, in unison they conveyed their conviction that he shouldn't waste his time and energy on such pursuits, inasmuch as he could get a nice job without an advanced degree.

Now they were reaping the rewards of their foolishness. His father, in desperation, conferred with me in search of answers. I knew him well enough to be very candid, but nonetheless approached our discussion diplomatically, without placing blame.

"He has a problem with dependence and motivation," I said. This came as no real surprise. "He obviously has never been encouraged to be on his own, work hard, and pursue his dreams."

He shifted uncomfortably, knowing well what his contribution to the problem had been.

I asked him if he had any solutions in mind himself.

"We've actually thought of selling the house to get both of them out," he replied. "I'm retiring next year. We have a small apartment near Naples, Florida, on the gulf. His mother and I have considered moving there."

It seemed like a drastic solution at first, especially for someone whose life's purpose had been to help his children avoid distress of any kind. But, on second thought, if it was something they had been thinking of anyway, perhaps it was not so drastic.

Basically, I had a great deal of confidence in his son. Even though he was handicapped in one way, he did possess many features of the resilient personality. I believed that, faced with the necessity of assuming more responsibility for himself, he would experience some distress but would make it in the end. He would probably welcome it enthusiastically. I shared my optimism.

"But what can we do in the meantime?" my friend inquired.

"It's hard, after a lifetime, to suddenly change tactics," I said, "but you'll have to, to some degree. You've told me he's unhappy about the way his life has been going. Why not sit down, calmly, rationally, and tell him that you've been unhappy about it too . . . not just because he's unhappy. There's too much concern nowadays about everyone's being happy, as if it were guaranteed in the Constitution. As I recall, the Bill of Rights talks about a guarantee to the pursuit of happiness, not happiness per se. Talk with him about it, because his unhappiness is a signal that something's wrong. And tell him what he already knows anyway, that part of what's wrong is that something's holding him back from making the most of his talents, and that something is that he's never gone on his own, learned to take risks and survive. If he gives you some blame for it, accept it. Assure him you've learned something yourself over the years. You can apologize if you want to, but basically focus on the positive, the now, and the future."

I thought of some practical steps he could take. I suggested he have his son contact a vocational guidance evaluation group, such as the one at Stevens Institute, in Hoboken, New Jersey, where professionals have been assessing vocational interest patterns and aptitudes for decades. They offer guidance to people of all ages, and they don't just deal with such issues as whether one would be more suited for an office job or for working in the wilderness as a forest ranger. When it's successful, such counseling also addresses itself to basic personality issues, such as motivation, something my friend's son quite clearly needed. I also suggested he explore the opportunities offered by the Outward Bound schools, white-water rafting, whaleboating off the coast of Maine, survival training in the mountains of North Carolina. Founded during the Second World War to train seamen to survive the sinking of their ships, the Outward Bound program has become a major resource for helping people of all ages develop many aspects of resilience.

"He also needs a mentor, someone older who can take an interest in him, teach him how to translate some of his dreams into reality, how to take risks. I'm afraid you've sort of disqualified yourself for that role, and present-day education being what it is, mentors have become an endangered species, so I doubt he came across any during his high school or college years. If he can't find it on his present job—which I think you'd know about if he had—he may have to look elsewhere for it, maybe another position more closely aligned to his basic interests."

"And what about his drifting from girl to girl?"

"I go back to my original point. If he can develop more independence, I'm sure that his relationships with women will fall into place. He may even be lucky enough to find a young woman who can not only love him but also help him live up to his promise."

Unfortunately, free advice is often disregarded as soon as it is offered, but my friend did not ignore what I had said. I was gratified to learn, as the months went by, that he followed my suggestions to the letter, adding a few ideas of his own. They did sell their home and move to Florida, but not until his son, after counseling, decided to enroll in graduate school three thousand miles away, in California, to study business entrepreneurship. Obviously, the young man's overall personality strengths had made it easier for him to face up to and deal with his limitations than it might have been had he been more extensively disabled by a serious lack of personal resilience.

Polarization is perhaps a good way to illustrate how personality traits can be so frozen as to block resilience. Persistently low self-regard is no more resilient than egotism; of course, it's more likely to make the unconfident person suffer than is its opposite, which is more likely to make the rest of us suffer. Excessive dependence is undoubtedly more debilitating than stubborn independence, but neither allows for much flexibility. Apparently, an accident on the highway is almost as likely for the excessively cautious driver as it is for the reckless or foolhardy one. The person who is Pollyannaish can be headed for disaster as easily as the one whose outlook on life is incessantly pessimistic.

We cannot come to terms with problems and solve them or find a direction in life if we're always scattered in our thinking or behavior; but by the same token, being obsessive about things, dwelling on problems, going over them again and again, following the extremely narrow track, is bound to bring us full circle, so that we end up where we began, nowhere. It might not be wise to laugh too heartily in the face of guards in a prisoner of war camp, but a perpetually grim outlook and an insistence on dealing with everything in life seriously and soberly can shut off our mental powers and significantly reduce our adaptability, making us incapable of resilience.

Too much gullibility can position us to buy one bridge after another, including the infamous one that spans the East River from Manhattan to Brooklyn, but a generally distrustful attitude will, besides winning us a reputation for being paranoid, seriously cut us off from important, potentially helpful human contacts altogether. Extreme privacy is no more a virtue than is spilling intimate secrets to the nearest stranger. Extreme suggestibility, being too easily influenced by others, is as disadvantageous as mental obstinancy.

The key to the resilient personality is, above all, flexibility: to be able to call on those particular strengths that are needed to meet particular challenges, to be logical and highly organized when logic and organization are called for, and to be able to be wildly illogical and even let things pass by undone in the interests of discovering unpredictable possibilities.

Of course, there are times when it may be impossible to avoid temporarily becoming polarized, especially during periods of extreme stress. In fact, some degree of polarization may be advantageous for a while. For example, you've lost your job or you've just ended a love relationship. You'll probably have to go out and find another job or another person with whom to share love. You may pull yourself sharply together and be quite aggressive in meeting such challenges. On the other hand, inaction may, paradoxically, be exactly what is called for, a period of doing nothing specific while you lean on others and collect your wits to reconsider the direction of your career or what kind of person you want to find and how to increase the odds of making a new relationship work more effectively. In the first instance, you will move toward independence; in the second, you may have to allow time to pass, during which you must learn to tolerate uncertainty and some measure of helplessness, while you brainstorm the options. Most importantly, you must be able to develop enough insight to know which course is demanded of you, as in the old prayer that asks God to give us the strength to change the things that can be changed, accept those that cannot, and the wisdom to know the difference.

However, once you've selected a strategic stance—action or temporary inaction—you must stick to it without becoming permanently fixed in your polarity. It's important to permit yourself to regain a healthy balance, just as it is important for you to try to keep yourself, in such times of stress, from becoming too afraid.

Panic is a major cause of immobilizing polarization. During times of disruption, many people, sensing that they are losing control over themselves and their environment (which they necessarily are), can be seized by intense fear, quite out of proportion to the particular stresses they are encountering and totally inappropriate, considering their basic abilities and resources to deal with these. Even as inflexibility will enhance your chances of panic, so, too, resilience itself will often save you from its clear and obvious perils.

Resilience is not a once-and-for-all thing. Our level of resilience will fluctuate over time. No one particular resilient attribute is a static ingredient of our personalities. Sometimes, for example, we are more courageous than at others. Moreover, because the traits that make up resilience may be present in varying degrees, some well developed, others not so, our overall level of resilience may be less than desirable. The presence of one strength does not guarantee the presence of another. You may, for example, possess a high level of self-esteem, but have little sense of responsibility; you may have a wide range of interests, but find it difficult to focus closely enough on one or two to pursue them effectively. What is important is that you periodically assess your strengths and limitations. Then, when you have the chance, play from strength, especially if and when you can personally choose your challenges. Meanwhile, with effort, you can work to develop those resilient attributes in which you seem to be deficient, so that you can improve your odds of dealing with future bifurcation points successfully. For, unfortunately, what skills and abilities we will need to face future periods of disruption is an equation we often cannot predict.

11

Biological Resilience

R ESILIENCE has an important physiological basis, too. When a patient's distress drags on and on in spite of the individual's obviously resilient personality and a supportive environment, I often must consider the possibility that some faulty biological mechanism is the culprit responsible for the persistence of the condition.

Stress induces physiological responses that accompany emotional and intellectual ones. One such response is the activation of hormones such as cortisol. When we are challenged, the pituitary gland, located near the brain and responsive to signals from it, excretes larger than usual amounts of a compound called the adrenocortical stimulating hormone, or ACTH. As a result, the adrenal gland, located near the kidney, increases its production of cortisol, a compound that, along with adrenaline, heightens the alerting and protective systems in the body. When stress passes, or as we adapt effectively to longer term stresses, hormone production diminishes, returning again to normal levels.

However, contemporary researchers have shown that in certain people subject to serious chronic depression, this endocrine system, once activated, does not seem able to turn itself off. Cortisol levels remain elevated. The suppression of hormone activity that should occur after the administration of a compound called dexamethasone fails to occur. What this implies is that the cycle of disruption and reintegration is blocked at a physiological level. Consequently, it may take an unduly extended period of time for the individual to recover from the impact of stress; or, in some instances, he may not recover at all without medical intervention.

Another hormone-producing gland involved in the stress response is the thyroid gland. People with overactive or underactive thyroid function usually have difficulty managing stress successfully until the physical condition has been adequately diagnosed and appropriately corrected.

More than twenty-five years ago, when I was director of the metabolic research unit at the Payne Whitney Clinic of the New York Hospital, my colleagues and I discovered fascinating evidence of a serious lack of biological resilience involving the thyroid hormone among certain psychiatric patients who had been disabled for years, people who were not unlike the thousands of homeless who inhabit our streets today. We found that patients who, for years, had been profoundly apathetic, socially withdrawn, and unresponsive to every treatment approach then available failed to show the more obvious physiological changes one would have expected (such as an outpouring of nitrogen in the urine) when they were given massive doses of a thyroid hormone. Although they did not show any evidence of thyroid disease as such, their bodies were as unresponsive and apathetic to this hormone as their overall behavior seemed to be to their environments. Either the thyroid hormone was being destroyed at incredible speed before it reached the tissues it was supposed to influence, or the tissues themselves were deaf and dumb to its message.

Today, the importance of calcium and other nutritional elements as part of a healthy diet is taken for granted. So is the importance of regular exercise, which, among other things, stimulates calcium retention. But years ago, when I was carrying out metabolic research, the professional climate for the most part considered nutrition in general and calcium in particular to be irrelevant to the human being's ability to cope with stress. What we discovered was that patients who were trapped in tenacious states of disruptive depression and who seemed unable to recover as a result of ordinary psychological therapy and rehabilitation alone were actually losing calcium from their bodies. When antidepressant drugs, such as imipramine, were used to interrupt the depression and restore well-being, the direction of calcium flow was reversed. As patients improved, they began to retain calcium in their bodies, particularly in their bone structures.

This research helped me to further refine the concept of the law of disruption and reintegration and the role of resilience in such transitions. It not only enabled me to look at what were called emotional disorders in a totally different light, but gave me an important new insight into the role of antidepressant drugs and similar agents in the treatment of people caught in depression.

For many patients, antidepressants accelerate the recovery from depression. In recent years, it has been shown that adding the salt lithium or small doses of the thyroid hormone to antidepressants can, when required, significantly boost their effectiveness. It has even been suggested that in certain situations, lithium alone can prove helpful. No longer do I think of or refer to the use of such agents as antidepressants. Rather, in ways that we still do not understand, I see them as resilience-enhancing drugs that act somehow, somewhere, to fill in a biochemical gap and, by putting the biological components of resilience in place again, allow the individual to call upon his own resilience to do the rest of the job of reintegration.

A most interesting dimension of resilience involves exposure of light. Recent experiments at the National Institute of Mental Health suggest that our ability to deal with stress can be significantly influenced by how much sunlight we expose ourselves to each day. A number of people seem to be better able to cope with change and challenge during the spring, summer, and early fall months; but as the days grow shorter and darker, they demonstrate a proclivity toward becoming lethargic, anxious, and depressed. These investigators exposed such vulnerable people to artificial broad-spectrum light for at least five hours a day and discovered that they could ameliorate or completely abolish their distress.

Obviously, this observation is but the tip of a deeply submerged iceberg. Plenty of people living in warm, sunny climates nonetheless lack resilience, but for some reason other than insufficient light. However, there is a curious relationship between where one lives, lifestyles, and behavior. Withdrawal in the face of conflict, keeping one's emotions to oneself, a propensity for depression are commonly seen among people living in northern climates, such as the Scandinavian countries. By contrast, people living on the Mediterranean coast, who appear to be more assertive, more expressive of feelings, and perhaps less prone to internalize conflict, seem less likely to become depressed in quite the same manner. Cultural influences (including the influence of religion) are so complex, however, that it would be utterly simplistic to attribute these differences exclusively to how much sunlight one ordinarily enjoys or the influence of light over many generations, but the fact does raise many provocative questions.

How might sunlight do all this? One possibility is that it activates vitamin D metabolism, which, in turn, exerts an effect on the metabolism of calcium in the body, a phenomenon we have already linked to resilience. There are undoubtedly other mechanisms at work as well. Perhaps one of the most interesting observations is that the sunlight influence seems to be mediated via the retina, in the eye. It is by looking at the light, not just being generally exposed to it, that one obtains the beneficial results.

Visual Perception and Resilience

During the past ten years, in collaboration with Dr. Melvin Kaplan, I have come upon another biological component of resilience that I believe to be especially significant, as it is easily measured and, if faulty, often easily rectified. This is visual perception. I have chosen to elaborate upon it in some detail because it is immediately useful and because, since the idea is still in the early stages of investigation and somewhat controversial, the reader may or may not hear much about it elsewhere for a time to come.

Our initial discoveries were made by happenstance, as many discoveries are. I asked Dr. Kaplan to evaluate a twenty-three-year-old woman who had been under psychiatric treatment for a decade. She had received a wide variety of psychiatric diagnoses, ranging from bipolar affective disorder to chronic hysteria, from borderline syndrome to schizophrenia, depending on what particular behavior patterns she manifested at any particular time and the orientation of the particular physicians assessing her condition. In spite of all that modern psychiatry had to offer, she spent most of these years in hospitals and halfway houses, never being able to recover sufficiently to resume and maintain a successful level of adaptation in the world.

I had heard of Dr. Kaplan through a mutual friend who was familiar with the work being carried out at the Gesell Institute in New Haven, Connecticut—a center dedicated to the study of childhood development. Dr. Kaplan had been a fellow there in developmental optometry.

Our hope that his examination of this patient might prove fruitful was very slight. Until then, his work had been largely confined to children with obvious visual problems and learning difficulties. But when all else had failed, I thought, why not give even the most remote possibility a chance.

What he found on his examination amazed all of us. The woman's visual perceptual abilities had seriously collapsed. The little she could see was seen as if through a narrow tunnel, linear, without depth, shutting out light or, at best, misdirecting it. She could barely organize the location and relationships in space of things around her. She could sustain the images she received for less than sixty seconds, unless she severely shrank the area she was viewing and concentrated on them intensely to keep them alive. She was, in effect, functionally blind.

Moreover, testing showed that the normal communication pathways between her visual systems and those systems in the lower centers of her brain and in her vestibular apparatus in the middle ear responsible for positioning her body in space, had been severely disrupted. Although she could, with some difficulty, follow moving objects with her eyes while sitting down, it was impossible for her to do so while standing up. Small wonder, then, that previous efforts to rehabilitate her had failed; each time she was confronted with the demands of the schoolroom or ordinary working environments, she would retreat in panic because of her total inability to cope with them.

The collapse of her visual perceptual systems had probably occurred when she was no more than three years old. Her family had noticed a change in her behavior at that time. She had become quiet and withdrawn, was terrified of the dark, and had considerable difficulty sleeping; subsequently, she did poorly in school, in spite of what appeared to be a high level of native intelligence. When she was thirteen, in the context of extreme stress (a death in the family and her parents' divorce), what little perceptual ability she had held on to vanished as she entered a state of emotional disruption from which she had, at the time of our assessment, not yet been able to recover.

She was given special directive lenses to wear regularly, which expanded her perception of the world around her. Systematic eye exercises designed to improve her ability to locate and organize objects in space were also prescribed. Over an eight-month period, this patient was gradually able to assume more and more responsibility for her own life. Now, more than ten years later, she is married, has children, holds a responsible job, and has not required any psychiatric care whatsoever.

Since then, we have studied several hundred men and women, some suffering with psychiatric conditions, many not. From these investigations, we have been able to create a hypothesis that serves as the basis for our continuing investigations.

Human beings have at least two visual systems. One is called the focal system. What we perceive around us is registered largely at the center of the retina, at the back of our eye. This image is then transmitted to the higher centers of our brain for identification and interpretation. This information answers the question

"What are we looking at?" It is essentially this focal system that our eye doctor examines when we go for a routine evaluation; if he prescribes glasses, he does so in order to make things clearer to us, at near vision or in the distance, so that we can more effectively see what it is that we are looking at.

There is, however, a second visual system that he does not investigate, as it is more the concern of the psychologist and neurophysiologist than of the ophthalmologist or optometrist. It is called the ambient system. Information that deals with where objects are located in the space around us and where we are positioned in relation to them and to the ground beneath us is also communicated from the eyes. But these data travel along different pathways, to our frontal lobe and to the lower center of our brain, which, in turn, interconnect with the vestibular apparatus in our ears.

It is a silent system. We are ordinarily not aware of its existence or operations. If it is not operating efficiently, it can produce stress and make it considerably more difficult to manage whatever stresses confront us. Yet, ironically, we would not usually be remotely conscious of our impairment, or if we were, we would not relate our distress to our visual perceptual systems until the problem had been demonstrated for us concretely in the course of a brief special examination.

In a random sampling of presumably healthy adults, more than twenty percent will show some degree of visual perceptual impairment; the incidence can rise to as high as seventy percent among people undergoing serious stress, especially if they are having a hard time dealing with it. We have concluded that the integrity of the ambient visual perceptual system is an important element in resilience. In fact, it may be one of the few aspects of resilience that lends itself to simple and objective measurement.

Perceptual flexibility can be tested by assessing the smoothness and facility with which we can adjust to the movement of objects toward our eyes (calling for convergence) and away from them (calling for divergence). How long can we keep something in focus—merging the separate images of each eye to form a single image—if it is moving toward us or away from us? Once fusion has been lost, how long afterward, and at what distance, will fusion return as the object moves?

The measurement of such flexibility seems to be an accurate way to determine how well we deal with stress and with the organization of space and what space contains around us. For example, once we have lost fusion as an object is being moved in either direction—toward us or away—we should, if we possess sufficient perceptual resilience, be able to regain a single, fused image within a short time span as its direction of movement is reversed. Should there be an inordinate delay in the restoration of the single, fused image, an important component of our resilience is probably defective and in need of correction.

How relevant visual perceptual systems may be to our ability to cope depends, of course, on many variables, not the least of which is the kind of life we lead and the responsibilities we assume. The demands on a farmer or woodsman in the outdoors are going to be quite different from those placed on the urban dweller, computer operator, flight control technician, or bank teller. The visual systems are, after all, a basic method of acquiring information from our environment. The greater the importance of information gathering, the more an impairment in perceptual function will interfere with a smooth, effective performance. Moreover, if we are perceptually dysfunctional, or become that way during a period of disruptive stress, the greater the role information processing plays in our lifestyle, and the more likely we are to be stressed and distressed by the details of everyday challenges and demands.

Resilience-restoring drugs; lenses and exercises aimed at correcting ambient visual perceptual flexibility; exposure to light, minerals, and other supplements, or a diet that is guaranteed to provide us with our nutritional requirements; regular exercise, such as walking and swimming; intelligently planned vacations; relaxation procedures—these are but a few of the approaches we now have available to help us deal with problems we may encounter in the biological dimensions of resilience and to keep those mechanisms in good, working order. But in a day and age when, by means of positron emission topography, we can visualize our brains in full color as we think, we must stand prepared for advances in medical research that will provide us with a great many surprises, and we will most likely be posed with new stresses that stem from the legal, ethical, and social consequences that such discoveries invariably bring with them.

1 2

Sources of Self-Esteem

BOUT EIGHTEEN years ago, at a small dinner party given by mutual friends, I had the privilege of meeting and talking with Sir Alec Guinness. He happens to be one of my favorite actors, so it was not difficult to compliment him on his work. I called to mind, among other roles, his part in the Broadway production of T. S. Eliot's play *The Cocktail Party*. Sir Alec played Sir Henry Harcourt-Reilly, a psychiatrist of sorts, profoundly wise, poetic, of course, and, perhaps, in keeping with the playwright's predilection, slightly mystical. I had seen the performance when I was a junior in medical school, a time when I was unsure what branch of medicine I would select for my specialty. Although I realized that everyday psychiatry was a far cry from that portrayed by Sir Alec, I could not help being influenced in my final decision by the role. I told that to Sir Alec. He seemed amused and genuinely pleased.

Many of the lines from *The Cocktail Party* have etched themselves in my memory. One such line occurred to me recently. Edward Chamberlayne, the attorney who has ended his affair with Celia Copplestone, says to Reilly: ". . . I am obsessed by the thought of my own insignificance." To that, Reilly replies:

Precisely. And I could make you feel important,
And you would imagine it a marvellous cure;
And you would go on, doing such amount of mischief
As lay within your power—until you came to grief.
Half of the harm that is done in this world
Is due to people who want to feel important.
They don't mean to do harm—but the harm does not
    interest them.
Or they do not see it, or they justify it
Because they are absorbed in the endless struggle
To think well of themselves.

I puzzled over those lines for years. It was only as I began to gain some understanding of the concept of resilience that I really began to feel I understood what Eliot was driving at. The regulation of self-esteem is what counts, not a perpetual state of self-satisfaction or discontent. Polarization implies that we have veered too much in one direction or another and that we have become fixed in a position of either persistently low self-regard or, at the opposite extreme, egotism. Rigidity and inflexibility are, as Eliot suggests, harmful, to the person himself and to those around him, however unintentional the harm may be. This is obviously so when it comes to those who are engaged in an insistent search for self-esteem, either because they have too little or because they need to preserve a sense of self that is grossly exaggerated; either extreme sets the stage for self-absorption and self-centeredness, which are difficult enough to bear, and outright selfishness, which to paraphrase Petronius in *Hamlet,* destroys both self and friend.

What, then, is the nature of healthy self-esteem? What part does its regulation play in the resilience process?

Maintaining and restoring self-esteem is a complicated phenomenon, filled with numerous important distinctions. There is yourself, as you view yourself, regardless of what skills you may have mastered or how others view you. Raw, fundamental, existential, emotional, conceptual, biological, you have formed a gut feeling about yourself during the earliest years of life. Whether you are inherently proud, worthy, and enthusiastic, or shameful, unworthy, and helpless will be determined to no small degree by how you have been brought up. Loving parents who praise you for what you do well and set limits on your behavior so that you don't hurt yourself, you eat your green vegetables, and you go to bed on time help a great deal in this process. Mastering skills—learning to tie your shoes and do your numbers and read *The Tales of Peter Rabbit*—adds a sense of competence and reinforces self-esteem. How others regard you as you reach out to engage the larger world of playmates and school affects your self-concept too.

What you have been striving to create (without realizing it) is a complex self-structure. Your perception of that structure must be reconfirmed periodically throughout the various stages of the life cycle. Adolescence, for example, is one of those times when a radical transformation in the regulation of self-esteem takes place. How the teenager views his or her body assumes a disproportionately great significance. Acceptance by peers seems a matter of life or death. Introspection emerges, leading to heightened self-consciousness and preoccupation with oneself. The teenager experiences wide swings in self-appraisal as he becomes much more reliant on a wider circle of other people whose opinions he values to help him define his own worth. This is the time to formulate a realistic picture of our assets and limitations, so that we can dream dreams and aspire to ambitions that legitimately suit our talents and potentials.

Hand in hand with the formation of self-esteem, we also create what psychiatrists have termed the superego, a place within each of us where our ethical and moral standards reside, where images of what we feel we should be and what we want to be reign, often in conflict with our appraisal of what and who we are. No person can always be or become what he thinks he should be. We will as frequently fall short of our target as achieve it. We will succeed. We will fail. And as we become adults, we will be repeatedly challenged by questions to which we will often have to find the answers all by ourselves, with less and less input from others. Am I a good husband or wife? Have I been a good parent?

Has my career been successful? Have I made my life count? Do I know how to regain self-respect after defeat?

I recall how vigorously Heidi Anderson struggled to resist my efforts to restore her self-respect. Heidi originally consulted me because she was depressed after an important love relationship had ended. She had hoped for marriage and was profoundly shocked and hurt to discover that her lover had never had any such intentions. She had long wanted to have a family of her own, but now, in her early thirties, she was beginning to feel that the chances of that coming to pass were fast diminishing.

Heidi was an attractive and accomplished young woman, with an enchanting smile, when she deigned to smile. She had majored in English at Brown University. For the previous seven years, she had been working as an editor for a leading publishing house in New York. But, in spite of numerous promotions and much praise from her superiors, she was convinced that she had neither talents nor special skills that would permit her to create a meaningful career.

"I wanted to be a writer. But since college, I've written nothing. I feel like a servant to other writers, not much more than a copy editor going over manuscripts and correcting typographical mistakes." I asked her if that was, in fact, her job. To the contrary, she reluctantly admitted, she had been the primary editor of several books that I had heard of and that had received critical acclaim.

Although the depression for which she had originally consulted me had abated within several months, she nonetheless persisted in her derogatory appraisal of herself. "I'm stupid, really," she insisted. "I had to work terribly hard all through school to get good grades. If I had been bright, I wouldn't have had to work that hard."

I had learned a long time before not to contradict frankly and directly a patient's insistence on low self-esteem. Such a strategy often intensifies his determination to prove to me how worthless he really is. So, in an offhand way, I said: "Even hard work wouldn't have won you those grades if you were really stupid." Then, shrugging my shoulders, I added, "But if you say so . . ."

Heidi did seem quite humorless. For her, life was a very serious business. Getting ahead was the goal, and it was to be achieved by mastery of detail, a tactic for which she paid a high price—forfeiting her spontaneity. Being a very private person, she also found it difficult to talk of her feelings and thoughts during our visits. She presumed that I would ask her what I wanted to find out and tell her what I wanted her to know. She also assumed that whatever I told her was calculated to make her feel better, whether I believed it or not. On the occasions when I complimented her about anything, she quickly dismissed such statements as "contrived." However, she was on the alert for criticism and could hear this even in my silences.

Her background offered me clues as to how Heidi had developed so little resilience in regulating her self-esteem. She was the only daughter in a family with three sons. She felt her parents had favored the boys whenever education or careers were discussed. Her father, who managed a local McDonald's franchise, had regarded her as his own "special little girl" when she was a small child. However, as she entered adolescence, he could not let her gracefully say her first good-bye, and subliminally perceiving the emergence of his daughter as a woman, he withdrew from her, completely ignoring her accomplishments in high school. She described her mother as a simple person, often helpless in her attitudes, very dependent on her husband, indecisive; she worked part-time as a courtroom stenographer. Her mother often cautioned Heidi not to set her sights too high in life, lest she be bitterly disappointed in the end.

"I had to shut them out," Heidi once shouted in a rare show of temper, covering her ears as if to prevent herself from hearing her own raised voice. "I'd come home with a straight-A report card. They'd look at it in a terrible hurry. Then they'd start talking about how one of my brothers had made captain of the basketball team or another had just been accepted at law school . . . But I've known this as long as I can remember. Knowing it doesn't change anything. They made me feel incompetent, and I can't get over it."

Heidi's problem with self-esteem had influenced her choice of boyfriends. The last two men she'd dated, including the one with whom she had broken up just before coming to see me, were quiet, unassuming men, lacking in humor or spontaneity themselves. One was an unsuccessful insurance salesman who was afraid to use the telephone; the other was a would-be artist who had yet to complete his first canvas and who seemed to deal with his own "endless struggle to think well" of himself by repeatedly putting Heidi down.

Heidi's insight into all this gave her some perspective. But it was not enough to induce meaningful change. Something more had to be done. I chose to play devil's advocate and attack the very foundation of her problem, her values, the intimate connection in her mind between achievement and self-worth. Even at the risk of angering her, I started to question why anyone should believe that it was necessary to accomplish anything in the world's terms in order to feel worthwhile.

At first, she thought my comments absurd. "Are you saying that because I'm a woman? You wouldn't say that to a man, would you?"

"Certainly. I don't think sex has anything to do with it. Don't you think we're all brainwashed into thinking that having a job and earning a living is the only way to get self-respect? Isn't that what keeps the economic cycle going? Mind you, that's not to say that people shouldn't work. Quite the contrary. Work's an essential part of living. But what I mean is that work is one thing, while self-esteem is something else."

"If self-respect doesn't come from achievement," she asked, "then where does it come from?"

Her question was so sudden and direct, she caught me off guard. I hesitated for a moment before answering.

"You see. You don't know the answer yourself," she said.

"When you first came to see me, Heidi," I said, "you were depressed. People who are depressed lose self-confidence. It's the name of the game. When they recover, most regain their own sense of worth. Others—like you—seem never to have enjoyed a reasonable amount of self-respect to begin with. Or if you did, you had to fight to hold on to vestiges of it in the face of a family that failed to appreciate your talents and abilities. By and large, you bought their low opinion of you and tied it in to the idea of being a woman. Accomplishment, you came to believe, was considered the prerogative of men, a thesis you adamantly and correctly refused to accept."

She gave me a skeptical look, one I had grown accustomed to seeing.

"Desperately seeking a sense of worth, you set out to succeed. But obviously, no amount of success filled the bill. You graduated from a first-rate college with honors. You've been employed and promoted in a highly competitive business. But you still haven't done enough to change the way you look at yourself. Maybe you're missing something altogether."

"What?"

I sensed that, perhaps for the first time, she had allowed me to get through her defenses and might actually be able to hear something positive about herself, and learn from it.

"You have a right to feel good about yourself regardless of how much money you make or whether the job you have right now lives up to all your expectations. I believe it's a right that all decent human beings should enjoy—to think well of themselves, as human beings."

"That's easy for you to say," she said. "You've already accomplished a lot."

"True. But I've failed sometimes too. Listen. One of the lessons I've learned the hard way is not to let my self-esteem stand or fall entirely on how well or poorly my patients fare."

"That sounds positively irresponsible."

"Not at all. Of course I care, a lot. But that kind of vulnerability would compromise my ability to be honest with you . . . to help you, or anyone."

My efforts to help Heidi excise her concept of who she was from what she did were beginning to work. The door was opening for her to reconsider what her talents really were and how she might best put them to use. As it happened, they weren't literary at all. Her desire to write was repeatedly frustrated by the fact that writing was not her strength; her real ability—and the reason she had won recognition from her superiors—was her ability to organize. In school, it was her skill in being able to distinguish between information that was important and that which was not that enabled her to obtain good grades. At her job, it was not her instinct for language that worked well for her; instead, it was her innate ability to set priorities, deciding what had to be done now and what could be postponed until later, combined with her passionate attention to detail.

Even Heidi had to admit that her managerial talents were real assets. The trouble was that she had placed no value on them. She used to feel that anyone could manage. Now she was beginning to admit that that might not be the case. "I enjoyed being the business manager of the college newspaper," she recalled, confirming the insight.

Heidi quit her publishing job and enrolled in a business administration course at Columbia. In our final session, I cautioned her that in years to come, she might suffer relapses and lose some of her newfound self-confidence. Such reversals were an inherent part of our response to disruptive situations. The issue was not whether she could hold on to self-esteem, but how quickly and effectively she would be able to regain it after humiliation, failure, loss, or other adverse life events temporarily robbed her of it. I recently received a postcard from her from Bermuda, saying that she loved school and had a new boyfriend, and that sometimes she felt she might really be OK.

We must keep in mind that self-esteem and its companion, self-confidence, are not static entities. They are not produced by some magical sense of superiority that enables us to go through life unscathed by life's reverses. Failure, whatever its nature, is bound to compromise how we see ourselves. Again, the key to the regulation of self-esteem is resilience, how fast and how effectively we can restructure ourselves after such stress.

In a sense, we can regard self-esteem as operating on several levels. There is the satisfaction we derive from a job well done. Not doing well at something that we consider important can and should cause us some dismay, and such discomfort ideally will motivate us to do better the next time around. There is the respect and praise we receive from friends, family, and coworkers; this is something we all need, although we must be on guard not to become addicted to it and must be prepared for long stretches in adult life when it may not be readily forthcoming.

Then there is the matter of values. Heidi Anderson's self-esteem was tied up with accomplishment. Although she was an attractive woman, her appearance meant nothing to her. Another person, however attractive, may never feel attractive enough and, hence, maybe vulnerable to low self-esteem. Still another may feel financially poor and consequently unaccepting of himself because his net worth does not exceed a million dollars. Still another, in spite of academic and professional success, may suffer with nagging self-doubts because she has never been able to become an accomplished athlete. Conceivably, a research scientist could win the Nobel Prize and still remain compromised with regard to self-esteem because he has never mastered the skills of sociability that he was told he must master from kindergarten on.

We must be able to identify our own values and consider how realistic they are in the light of our abilities, opportunities, and actual life situations, so that we can bring into better balance the distance between what and who we are and what and who we want to be.

Nor is there anything wrong with being dissatisfied with ourselves. Distress is a key motivator for learning. As one forty-three-year-old man put it to me: "I've always handled money badly. I'm a teacher. When I went into this profession, I did it because I felt I'd love the work. I did. But I never paid any attention to money. I put my paycheck in the bank and paid my bills. That seemed simple. But with kids growing up, and inflation, I suddenly find I haven't enough money, and I don't know what to do about it. I lie awake at night worrying. It makes me feel like a failure, as if I've wasted my life, sidestepped opportunity, been lured into becoming absorbed in work that could never give me what I need."

"It's never too late to learn," I advised him. "Take some courses in money management. Look at your budget. There's nothing wrong and everything right about taking care of yourself and your family. It doesn't mean you have to care less about your work. It's just that focusing on money is something you never did before. You can find solutions once you stop castigating yourself about this."

Accepting our ignorance is part of resilient self-esteem regulation. I recall sitting in the university hospital cafeteria once, having lunch with several colleagues, including a former director of psychiatry. Someone brought up a name and the piece of research that that person was carrying out. An article about it had appeared in a recent medical journal. I believe it involved immune systems and their possible involvement in depression. My field was depression, but I was not familiar with this particular line of inquiry.

"What work is that?" I asked.

The director seemed startled and looked in my direction disapprovingly. Several others mumbled.

"Well, I had a choice," I said. "I could sit here and pretend that I knew what you were referring to. But then, I wouldn't learn what it was all about, would I? Tell me, how many of you actually were not familiar with this research either?"

Only one of the seven raised his hand, although three more later acknowledged their ignorance privately to me.

Being able to admit that you don't know something or can't do something is a vital part of resilient self-esteem regulation. Here are a few other guidelines. Remember the child's story of the little train chugging up the mountain, puff by puff? The engine kept saying, over and over again: "I think I can, I think I can, I can, I can, I can." Conditioning yourself to think positively is a good start.

Take each day and each task as it comes. One of the cardinal rules we physicians follow in helping people who have had major episodes of emotional disruption to gradually regain confidence in themselves is to identify specific jobs they can carry out successfully within the limitations of their current disabilities. The technique involves restoring a sense of competence by doing what you are capable of doing now. For instance, suppose you're a real estate broker. For some reason, you don't have the energy to get on the phone or out of the house on a particular day. Maybe, then, you should simply stay home, sit down at your desk, and do nothing more than make a list of prospective clients whom you will call on another time, when you feel more vitality. No one expects a person recovering from hip surgery to go out and run the marathon the first week out of the hospital. If disruption has forced you to crawl, crawl; later, you'll be able to walk.

Play from strength, which implies that you know and have learned to deal with your weaknesses.

Don't suffer humiliation when life forces you into contact with failure, for humiliation delays learning and recovery. Of course, if you can learn to laugh a little at yourself, so much the better. As Sir Henry Harcourt-Reilly tells Edward Chamberlayne:

It will do you no harm to find yourself ridiculous . . .
You will find that you survive humiliation
And that's an experience of incalculable value.

Most of us are vulnerable to others' opinions of us. We should seek and be open to constructive criticism, but discriminately, paying attention to input that is legitimate and passing off that which is destructive. Not listening can be as serious a limitation as being too susceptible to the influence of others. To the extent that it is possible, we should make every effort to surround ourselves with people with whom we share mutual respect and minimize our involvement with those who repeatedly provoke or diminish us. In assessing those around us, we should consider a set of obvious questions. Does our boss commend us on jobs well done, or do we only hear from him when things go wrong or, worse yet, when he is in a bad mood and *believes* they have gone wrong, regardless of the facts? Are we married to a man or woman whose attitude seems to be supportive, or one dedicated to the deflation of our hopes and only too ready to remind us of our shortcomings? Have we, like survivors of prisoner of war camps, learned how to maintain our self-respect in the face of the enemy? Have we an escape plan in mind?

For most of us, a sense of community is also a vital part of sustaining our self-esteem. It has to do with identity. People can more readily keep in mind who they are and respect themselves when those around them seem to know and respect them too. Throughout the world, however, the traditional sources of one's sense of community and identification are threatened by change. The immigrants who came to the United States created a community among themselves, sharing the same language and customs; but the homogenization of America is rapidly eradicating that community. The very architecture of the buildings in which we live is making our interactions with others more problematic. In Britain, for example, a study of high-rise living showed that the taller the buildings in which people live, the less likely it is that they will acknowledge each other's existence and afford neighborly recognition and support.

You'll probably have to learn to build your own community, by chance or by design. One of my daughters, for example, is the mother of twins; she has found a community with other mothers of twins. Some of you will find it on the golf course or the tennis court; some, by going to the same summer resort each year; some, with colleagues at work. But it is growing harder and harder, as people become more mobile and as the landmarks that provided our civilization with a sense of continuity are vanishing.

1 3

Developing Autonomy

L EARNING that we are separate beings and not part of
our mother is one of the earliest creative realizations we
come to during the first year of life. The rest of childhood
is spent developing competence, various skills, and a stronger
sense of ourselves. It is a time when even the least of us shows a
proclivity for invention. Learning to tie a shoelace, eat with a
spoon, or find one's way home from school—although these will
rapidly become habitual, mindless actions—are initially quite
creative and derive from and strengthen one's growing sense of
autonomy.

The search for autonomy is a recurrent odyssey throughout
the course of the life cycle. At first, it takes place within one's own
family. Later, it extends to playmates and teachers. We assume that
this evolution will continue until, at last, we reach a point called
maturity, when we put on academic caps and gowns, are handed
pieces of paper called diplomas to confirm our autonomy, and told
to be on our way to meet the challenges life holds in store for us.
Often, by then, both our autonomy and the creative initiative that
it embodies have been seriously compromised by what we have
been exposed to; we find it hard to think for ourselves, and we remain vulnerable to the standards and values of our peers.

Let us use an eraser to illustrate metaphorically the struggle that confronts us throughout life in our efforts to preserve autonomy.

I sit at a small desk in a schoolroom. In my hand, I hold the only eraser there. Being foresighted, I had thought ahead to bring it with me this morning.

How does my teacher respond to my precocity? Instead of praising me, she leans over and whispers in my ear that awful word: "Share." It's really not a bad idea, but I want to shout: "It's my eraser!" I don't. Instead, I hand it to the little girl sitting at the next desk. She smiles. Suddenly, I feel much better. Her glance is my reward. I have given up a bit of my autonomy, but that seems all right. I feel good. One hopes this event will not condition me in years to come to give away everything, or other symbolic possessions, more valuable than erasers, or even a part of my soul, in return for an equally enchanting smile.

Preserving autonomy (as represented by my eraser) will continue to be a challenge as innumerable life situations arise that threaten to rob me of mine.

Dogmatism: "We have all the answers. You have none. Erase the contrary images you have in your mind."

Business: "If you give me your eraser, I'll pay you a higher rate of interest than you can get elsewhere."

Power struggles: "This is the War of the Erasers. Winner takes all."

Murder: "They killed him for nothing more than an eraser."

Peer pressure: "If you want to be one of the group, you'll have to throw your eraser away, just as the rest of us have."

Marriage: "If you want us to get along, you'll just have to put that eraser in the attic and leave it there for good."

Control: "You want this eraser, don't you. All right. Reach out for it. Ha! You didn't get it that time, did you? Try again. Oops! Almost got it. That's it. Now, beg."

Addiction: "I can't go on living without it. So, here, take my eraser in exchange, and give it to me."

Criticism: "You're a rotten person. You won't give me your eraser. You don't even know how to use it. Look. You've smudged the page, you fool."

Seduction: "I can't tell you how much I admire someone with an eraser . . . and you know how to use it so well. Not a pencil mark left on the page. Now, since you don't need it any more, why not give it to me, sweetheart?"

There is no time in life other than youth when we enjoy a sense of forever and seemingly unfettered personal freedom. You have a few dollars in your pocket, enough perhaps to buy a plane ticket to Australia to see for yourself what the Outback is like. You may have a girlfriend or boyfriend, maybe two, but nothing serious. You have, it seems, all the time in the world. You may not even be concerned about purchasing a return ticket.

"That's the way I felt when I was twenty-two," George Bistrom told me. "I wish I could feel that free again."

I met George at a corporate training session on stress management I gave several years ago. He asked if he could speak with me privately after the evening discussion.

"I'm forty-two. I feel weighed down by everything. Burned out . . . and trapped. I can't save. Every cent I make goes out to meet the monthly bills. I feel I'm not going anywhere in my job, but I can't risk leaving. I've been having a lot of trouble sleeping, and I get headaches my doctor can't find any reason for. How can I approach anything creatively, like you were saying in your talk tonight?"

George was the company's assistant personnel director, a man with both feet solidly placed in middle age. He had a wife, three children, a mortgage on his three-bedroom town house built in what had once been a potato field, two cars, and a membership in a country club. He spent an hour and a half driving to work each way, listening to the news radio station repeat the same headlines every twenty-two minutes. "Give us a few minutes of your time and we'll give you the world," the announcer promised. George would squeeze his fingers around the steering wheel and inch toward the next toll booth. Up at six-forty-five in the morning and arriving home at seven-thirty in the evening, he usually went to bed at ten. He could only call weekends his own; but much of those were spent shoveling snow in the winter and raking leaves in the fall, interspersed with Saturday night dinners with friends and tennis on Sunday mornings, when the courts weren't packed. George and his wife, Lorna, rarely made love any more. There was not enough privacy and very little interest.

One thing that George Bistrom had always been greatly concerned about was how others regarded him. It gave him a sense of pride to own his home and belong to the club. He felt important when he said he worked for an electronics firm, as if he were part of the leading edge of new technology. He enjoyed the idea that people regarded Lorna as a particularly attractive woman. He obtained much of his self-esteem from his surroundings, and, to maintain it, he had steadily forfeited all but the last vestiges of his autonomy.

"I don't stand up for anything or to anyone any more, the way I used to when I was young," he said. "Not that I'm faced with any real problems. One, maybe. The new personnel chief. He took the job around eight months ago."

That, I noted, was about the time George's insomnia and headaches had begun.

"He's the kind of guy you never know where you stand with. No praise. No criticism. Nothing. Last month, out of the blue, he pink-slipped two people and dumped them, just like that. No warning. No explanations. I'm embarrassed to admit this, even to you . . . but it scares me."

"I suppose it should," I said. "You probably could get another job nowadays. Nobody likes change. On the other hand, your whole life structure could be turned upside down, and you might have to make major changes."

"How could I? At my age? What would I do?" I noted a tone of panic in his voice.

I thought of millions of Georges, living in suburbia, working for all kinds of organizations, who unwittingly might have traded their psychological freedom for filet mignon, an Audi, and membership in a country club. Having become so strongly dependent on their life structures, they had grown to believe that they could not survive in any other way of life.

"You feel helpless to do anything about this?" I asked him. He didn't reply, but I could see that he was struggling with unexpressed anger.

"If you're angry about this, why not admit it . . . at least to yourself?" I asked.

"How could you understand? You're a doctor. You're in charge of your own life. You don't have to answer to anyone."

I smiled. "Do you want to hear the long list of people, organizations, licensing boards, and all the rest I'm accountable to? I could lose my structure of independence as quickly and as surely as you feel you have. But true autonomy isn't simply a matter of whether you're living and working within an organization of some kind or in business for yourself. It's a state of mind. It's how you feel about yourself and yourself in relation to everything around you."

The conditions under which George worked were not unlike those found in many other contemporary organizations in the private and public sectors of the economy. In fact, his were better than most. Independence of thought and action are commonly discouraged. The rules tell you not to stick your neck out. Don't get embroiled in conflict. If something goes wrong, hide it, or better yet, fix the blame on someone else.

Procrastinate until it's no longer possible; then try to solve problems with last-minute crash programs. If you get too many letters, don't answer them, but don't stop writing memos. The same goes for phone calls, unless they're from your boss, a key client, or your wife. And get your secret hostilities out by making people wait for appointments. Above all, never make decisions without being sure everyone who matters ever so slightly has been consulted and approves.

George's world was not designed to be a prison. His superiors would have laughed in amazement if the word *prison* had been used to describe their luxurious glass offices that overlooked gardens and fountains and their ultramodern cafeteria that served a choice of three entrées at lunch every day. How could an organization that sends you to training conferences on stress management and other vital topics at Hilton Head or in Palm Springs twice a year be considered a prison? Weren't the rewards for giving up your freedom sufficiently attractive? Wasn't there safety in numbers? How could you believe for a moment that executives' succumbing to alcoholism or dropping dead of heart attacks in their early fifties had anything to do with the conflict between their wish for personal independence and their need to collaborate with systems that make it hard for them to think and act independently?

I used an old tactic called the worst-case hypothesis. "Ask yourself, what's the worst thing that could happen? You might get fired. Then you'd have to sell your home and scale down for a while, look for another job, maybe retrain yourself. You'd have to swallow some pride and ask a few friends for help. Maybe your wife would have to go back to work. You might have to relocate. You could even drive a bus."

"Drive a bus!"

"You could, if you had to. But I mean that figuratively rather than literally. Driving a bus means you know that somehow, some way, you can survive."

I asked George to give me more particulars about the nature of his work, and discovered that he had not been as deprived of autonomy as he had thought himself to be. To be sure, there were ordinary insecurities and frustrations, as there are in all work situations. But his feeling of being thwarted and diminished as a person was as much perceived as real. For example, one of his responsibilities involved searching out new ways to evaluate prospective employees. Another dealt with developing more sophisticated methods to assess work performance. When I showed a genuine excitement for the possibilities inherent in these assignments, George seemed surprised at first, and slightly incredulous. But as we talked, he began to see for himself that there were opportunities and challenges available to him. Within the limitations of his authority, there was a good deal he could initiate on his own. And if he had to sell his ideas within the company, that, too, could be a chance for him to regain autonomy and employ imaginative strategies to succeed, rather than succumb to a sense of helpless futility and the resultant stagnation. He recalled that under his high school yearbook picture, his classmates had placed a quotation from Shakespeare: "soft-spoken, tactful, and exceeding wise." Diplomacy was indeed one of George's strong points, one he could use to cushion the effects of his taking more initiative.

George Bistrom was an organization man. He was not suited to be anything else. He needed structure within which to function. What he had to figure out was how he could sustain autonomy, given that context.

At the opposite pole from the organization man is the entrepreneur, a person who represents raw autonomy. You can often trace his initiative, imagination, willingness to march to the beat of a different drummer, to the far reaches of his childhood, when he was selling lemonade in front of his house or organizing the neighborhood youngsters to paint garages and rake leaves. While others were making their plans for graduate school or rushing to interviews with the Fortune 500 companies, he was trying to decide whether to rent a barn where he could work on his inventions or try his hand at real estate development. A twelve-hour workday is his norm. Energetic, restless, determined, he is driven by ambition, talent, a sense of destiny, and the desire to be rich or, perhaps, to be a saint. His strengths are persistence and creative power.

In contrast to George Bistrom, who seemed so vulnerable to such issues as status and position in life and was too easily influenced by family, friends, and coworkers, the entrepreneur suffers with a different kind of vulnerability. He often has too much of a good thing and risks uninvolvement. He may not heed potentially valuable advice. In business, he often finds it difficult to adapt to structure once the idea he has created, developed, financed, and marketed successfully has matured to the point that a management team who require structure become necessary for its further growth and survival. In his personal life, he risks being impulsive—in love, among many other things—and he may be quite limited in his ability to relate with and accommodate to the needs of those around him.

Most of us fall somewhere along a spectrum that extends from intense autonomy at one extreme to being seriously dependent, lacking a mind and will of our own, at the other. Autonomy, like all psychobiological systems, must be elastic. There are times when we must ignore the input of others to protect our creative powers; then there are times when we must be able to reach out for the support and advice we need. There are times for action, and there are times when we must wait for a sign—from events as they evolve, or as an illumination arising from our own unconscious minds, which we have learned to access.

Autonomy is a critical ingredient in the creative process and, hence, in resilience. The practice of creative strategies will help us keep our autonomy alive, even in the later part of our lives, when circumstances often conspire to push us back toward a state of relative helplessness again.

14

Creativity

C REATIVITY is an essential part of resilience for two obvious reasons. First, at bifurcation points, things are a shambles and the outcome is quite unclear. Second, when the pieces are reassembled, we, or our lives, or both, will assume new and unfamiliar homeostases.

I have had over the years the unique opportunity to meet and correspond with a number of outstanding scholars who have studied and written about the nature of the creative process. All of them have acknowledged that creativity is a very difficult thing to define. However, there is some general agreement.

The creative act does not create something out of nothing. It rearranges, combines, synthesizes already existing facts, ideas, and frames of reference. Most agree that it does not follow the rules of ordinary logic; instead, it is rooted in an irrational way of thinking, with emotional and intellectual forces beyond consciousness playing vital roles. The creative act clearly adheres to the law of disruption and reintegration, reflecting, and perhaps an inherent part of, something innate in the biological structure of human beings or even all nature.

Arthur Koestler's classic description of the creative experience sounds like the very heart of successfully transiting a bifurcation point. In *Act of Creation,* he wrote that the creative person must "plunge into a 'dark night of the soul' before he can reemerge into the light. The history of the sciences and arts is a tale of recurrent crises, of traumatic challenges, which entail a temporary disintegration of the traditional forms of reasoning and perception . . . followed by the liberation from restraint of creative potentials, and their reintegration in a new synthesis."

In its broadest sense, creativity can be defined as a response to a situation that calls for a novel but adaptive solution, one that serves to accomplish a goal. Usually, when life presents us with a problem, we will approach it in accordance with the abilities, habits, and skills that have enabled us to find solutions to similar problems in the past. When the same task is repeatedly encountered under rather monotonous conditions in the same kind of setting—preparing breakfast, catching the commuter train, cleaning and reorganizing the living room, making the seventeenth sales call of the day, watching the evening news on television—our responses become stereotyped, imprisoned in rigid patterns. This is why it is so difficult for marketing experts to get us to abandon our favorite brand of toothpaste or our favorite TV news channel in favor of the one they are promoting.

However, when the challenges of change reach a point where they contain serious new elements that make it impossible to solve them by the same old rules of the game, we feel helpless, perhaps even hopeless for a time, unless and until we can find a new set of rules to combine with those we already know in order to come upon resolution. To unlearn old strategies in favor of new ones is stressful, which is why adaptability becomes harder as we grow older. By then, we have accumulated a veritable attic of obsolete responses, and we risk being convinced that what we have learned already is as much as we need to know.

All those who have studied the subject believe that the unconscious plays a crucial role in the unlearning-relearning process and the discovery of new dimensions. Whether it is accurate to separate our unconscious mind into various compartments or not is a debatable issue. It seems we all have a deeper unconscious, an area made up of powerful, stereotyped, very unoriginal perceptions and emotions that date back to the earliest stages of our lives. This part of our unconscious is frequently associated with enormous reservoirs of anger and fear; consequently, if its hold is too powerful, it can block access to the other, more constructive region of the unconscious, called the preconscious.

The preconscious mind, a level of the unconscious much closer to consciousness, is apparently directly involved in creative thinking. Here, unencumbered by the restrictions of everyday language and compelling logic, we are able rapidly to mobilize large amounts of data, make otherwise irrational connections, and superimpose ingredients that are quite dissimilar into new perceptual and conceptual patterns. We are continuously exposed to a vast amount of incoming information through our senses; only a small proportion of it will be actively remembered. This must be so, as much of our conscious activity must be directed toward dealing with everyday matters at hand, and if our attention could not be selective, we would drown in the noise of the universe. The preconscious is not unlike the hard-disk drive of a computer, where the contents of all past experiences are registered and remain to some degree available for access if and when we need them, as long as we know the retrieval code. However, unlike the computer bank, which is totally inert and at the command of the machine's operator, these imprints have a life of their own. No matter how long ago they may have been stored there, they can influence how we think and feel now, and even during our search for creative solutions, involving the activity of the preconscious is more like a collaboration than a command performance.

Psychologist Carl Jung added another dimension of understanding to the role the unconscious may play in creativity. By introducing his concept of a collective unconscious, Jung saw the unconscious mind as more than a data bank and information processor. The center of his formulation was "archetypal sources." He postulated the presence of an objective psyche (in contrast to that part of the unconscious that is made up of each person's unique past experiences); this aspect of the unconscious possesses imprints that are universal to all human beings, carried forward from generation to generation by some means, perhaps genetically. It contains the essence of human experiences through the ages that have been formative enough to be permanently, although not unalterably, registered on the cells and pathways of our brain structure. This objective psyche expresses itself through visual imagery—symbols that circumvent the restrictions of language and do not conform to any basic logic. What is expressed thereby reflects those elements of human history that have served the purposes of personal and species survival and evolution, such as nurturing, self-assertion, a sense of community, love, God.

It appears, unfortunately, that the ability to think and act creatively involves skills that are suffocated in many of us as we grow up in families that discourage originality, as we are educated in school systems that demand intellectual conformity to what is being taught, as we end up working in organizations that dispel any hope of imaginative planning and execution. In fact, many of us have been taught to disregard creativity altogether and to be suspicious of those who explore its mysteries or advocate its value. There was a time when creativity was actually thought to be a sign of madness. Sigmund Freud, who in one of his many dogmatic assertions held creativity to be little more than a substitute for other, more basic physical satisfactions, such as sexual fulfillment, did little to help the cause.

Another source of confusion lies in the incorrect assumption that creativity must manifest itself in some unique talent and be expressed through artistic endeavors or scientific discoveries, rather than in the context of ordinary living. Then, too, one may ask: How can you say that creativity has anything to do with planning our lives and coping with stress when so many people, famous and otherwise, with great creativity in some particular area have seemed unable to keep their lives in order or cope with conflict competently—the Judy Garlands, the Richard Burtons, the Edgar Allan Poes. To begin with, being creative is a pivotal factor in resilience, but it is by no means the only one. Moreover, some people compartmentalize their creativity, especially when it is associated with an unusual talent; they express it through very few channels and fail to integrate it with their overall approach to life. Still others are addicted to the disruptive phase of the creative cycle, prolonging chaos and, in fact, seeking it out in preference to entering into the reintegrative phase, which can bring with it a new level of homeostasis and, for a while, a period of significant peace and coherence. And finally, as Shakespeare noted in *Hamlet,* a person can suffer from a "particular fault," not necessarily of his own doing, which, in the end, does him in. For example, some of us are pulled toward helplessness, an excessive need to depend on others most of the time, and, as a result of this, the effective employment of creative energies in any sphere will be blocked.

Psychological testing of creative individuals has clearly shown a close connection between creativity and our ability to deal with stress. On the Minnesota Multiphasic Personality Inventory, for example, creative people show significantly low scores for a wide spectrum of tendencies associated with poor coping abilities, such as hysteria, paranoia, and social introversion. Other studies have shown that creative people possess a higher than average quantity of traits commonly associated with ego-strength, such as dominance, responsibility, self-control, tolerance, intellectual efficiency, an openness to feelings and ideas, and a wide range of interests. Flexibility and the mingling of characteristics that the larger population often regards as contradictory are prominent features of such personalities. Creative men, for instance, are able to combine traditionally masculine attitudes, such as aggressiveness and competitiveness, with traditionally feminine ones, such as sensitivity and empathy. Creative women seem to do the same, being able to express themselves spontaneously and assertively, working at jobs once considered the exclusive territory of men, without forfeiting their nurturing abilities and compassion.

Being able to think creatively and approach problems in an imaginative way is an inherent part of resilience. Moreover, there is every reason to believe that learning to acquire and practice proven methods of stimulating creativity will substantially enhance our resources to cope with stress.

1 5

Learning to Think Creatively

T HE ABILITY to think and act creatively is a universal human strength. Of course, there is wide variability in the amount of creative potential that each of us possesses, as well as in the degree to which we have developed this potential. There is also considerable difference with regard to the extent to which we have been able to integrate creativity with other essential ingredients of resilience, such as the ability to tolerate distress and the discipline to pursue well-defined goals.

Nonetheless, the intimate relationship between creativity and resilience is such that the more we master creative problem-solving skills the more we will be able to respond to stressful situations resiliently. At first, our efforts to employ creative tactics may seem labored, even artificial. But with practice, these can become a basic part of our spontaneous response to challenge.

Stages in the Creative Problem-Solving Process

Creative problem solving takes place in five stages, which involve a delicate blending of logical and illogical thought processes. These stages vary in length and intensity with the issues that confront us. They do not always have to follow each other in strict sequence. Sometimes, a particular stage may require considerable time and thought; sometimes, one can move through it with lightning speed.

The first stage is fact-finding. Here, one reexamines the situation to gain as much information about it as possible. Any significant life problem deserves such attention, whether the question is what career direction to choose, why one is still single at thirty-one when getting married and having a family has always been a goal, how to renew a troubled marriage, or what to do with oneself after retirement.

The second is problem finding, in which one redefines issues, trying to see them in a new light. For example, a problem in deciding on a career path may really be rooted in an inability to divorce oneself from parental expectations; marriage conflicts may stem more from a failure to handle the demoralizing influence of in-laws than from the quality of the relationship with the person to whom one is married.

The next stage is idea finding, wherein one generates options as stimulated by the problem as it is now freshly viewed. For example, having explored the question of why one is still not married at thirty-one and redefined the issue as a fear of intimacy, one begins to think of new ways to improve the ability to relate to others—encounter group experiences, developing recreational interests such as skiing or tennis that can be shared with others, attending courses to develop self-confidence and social skills. Or, if the question of what to do after retirement has been redefined as what interests one had as an adolescent or young adult and has neglected in the years since, one may look back to those earlier times for valuable ideas.

The fourth stage is solution finding, in which one exerts judgment to evaluate the meaning and both the positive and the negative consequences of the ideas that have been produced. Now we are moving back to a more logical appraisal of options. Skiing and playing tennis would bring one in contact with more people and increase one's chances of meeting someone special; however, if one is not that competitive, skiing would seem to be the better choice of the two. Moreover, since the real problem appears to be a fear of closeness, an encounter group experience or counseling would seem to be the most relevant course to pursue early on. Or again, having recognized that the negative effect of in-laws has been disrupting one's marriage, and having considered a variety of ideas that range from belligerent confrontation to total avoidance, one may decide that the best course of action seems to be a heart-to-heart talk with one's husband or wife to shape a foreign policy to deal with the relatives jointly and more effectively.

The final stage is acceptance finding, wherein one develops the best ideas as fully as possible and proceeds to test them in the real world. Here, planning, initiative, and self-discipline are called into play.

Two Critical Guidelines

Two vital guidelines for creative problem solving that apply to each stage in the process and that most of us ignore or violate regularly are the rule of deferred judgment and the rule that quantity leads to quality. It goes against the grain to withhold premature criticism during our search for ideas and to try to come up with as many ideas as we can. These two tactics, however, are important, as the ideas we come up with at first will usually be more stereotyped than those that emerge later on and afford us little by way of new insights. We all tend to jump in and analyze and criticize our own (as well as others') ideas as soon as they have been expressed. We have a natural tendency to limit the solutions we think of to a pitiful few. How about taking a vacation without the children, for example? Not enough money. Besides, there's no one to stay with them. How about finding a way to facilitate a promotion in the company? There's no point in even trying. It's all politics anyway. While the negatives may have a kernel of truth in them, bringing them up, one by one, as each new idea appears, automatically blocks the entrance of new, better, and more suitable options.

With few exceptions, we are all somewhat subject to the pressures of conformity, caught up in our present perception of reality, which has been formed and protected by habit and experience. We all fear new ideas that are too far out of the ordinary. We don't want to seem foolish, even if only to ourselves. Those of us with a long-standing vested interest in being out of the mainstream of thinking and behavior are no exception—we, too, can be thwarted in our creative efforts by an unimaginative adherence to nonconformity.

Keeping in mind these two particularly important rules, we can also learn to master certain approaches that have been shown to increase our chances of seeing things in a new light, some of which serve to put us in touch with the valuable resources of our unconscious.

The Power of Language

One of the basic strategies used to discover new solutions is to change the language in which we think and with which we express our ideas. The word *creativity* itself, for example, touches basic assumptions that may seriously block our ability to use creative skills to deal with stress.

Consider the words people use to describe their encounters with disruption. They are most often judgmental, to say the least. "This is not a manly way to behave." "Fear is the sign of a coward." "I should have done this or that sooner—only a fool would wait so long." "Depression means I'm weak." These are only a few of the self-criticisms that profoundly delay reintegration.

I have often given serious consideration to the potentially crippling effect of medical terminology on the speed and certainty with which patients may recover from such episodes. The very words and attitudes professionals convey to patients and patients then use to define themselves can seriously delay recovery. Diagnosis is, in many ways, destiny.

Rebecca Holt is now nineteen years old. She is in her first year of college, in the first quarter of her class. Rebecca is an attractive, sociable young woman with a wide range of interests. She has a boyfriend. But things have not always been this way for Rebecca. When she was fourteen, she spent nearly a year in a psychiatric institution, where she carried the diagnosis schizophrenia.

A few weeks before her hospitalization, Rebecca's parents had separated. Her mother and father were both attorneys. She was their only child. For weeks, she had lain awake at night, frightened, unable to sleep, listening to their incessant arguing in the room next to hers. One morning, she simply did not get out of bed to go to school. Alarmed, her mother called their pediatrician, who suggested she try to persuade Rebecca to accompany her to a psychiatrist for consultation. Rebecca refused. Holding her lips tightly together, her fists clenched, she sat in bed, staring into space, refusing to acknowledge that she had even heard her mother speak.

The psychiatrist came to the house. In fact, he came almost every day. But Rebecca would not answer his questions. She would not eat, or read, or watch her favorite shows on television. Not certain whether he was dealing with the onset of a serious psychiatric disorder, and feeling unable to control the situation at home, the doctor recommended hospitalization. Reluctantly, Rebecca's parents concurred.

I was asked to see her six months later, after she had apparently been through a stormy course of ups and downs there, without any substantial improvement.

"I'm never going to get better," she told me. When I asked her why she felt that way, she answered: "Because I'm schizophrenic, and schizophrenics don't get better."

It had not required outstanding detective work for Rebecca to discover the diagnosis assigned her by the staff, tentative though it may have been. There were days on end during which she would not speak. Several times she had to be tube fed because she would not eat. Once, she struck out at a nurse who turned the radio off when she was listening to it in the lounge; she was placed in a windowless, furnitureless seclusion room for the rest of that day.

What was quickly apparent to me was that Rebecca, having been, for all practical purposes, a child at the time of her admission, had no reference point from experience with which to evaluate what she was going through. Seeing how some of the other patients behaved, she thought it amusing at times to imitate them; she also did so to get attention. Most importantly, she did so because she felt, sometimes, that disturbed behavior was expected of her. After all, she deduced, she was mentally ill.

"What if you are not mentally ill?" I asked her. She looked at me. "What if you simply fell apart when your home fell apart? And what if, just like your parents, you have to put your life together and you've been finding it hard to do that?"

"If I'm not mentally ill, then what am I doing here?" she asked, logically. "And how come they think I'm an incurable schizophrenic?"

"Maybe you've been acting like one without being one," I suggested. "Then again, maybe there's no such thing as schizophrenia. Maybe it's just a word that we doctors use to lump patients with certain symptoms together so that we can talk with each other about them."

After a few minutes of silent thought, she said: "If that's true, maybe I could get better."

I often try to restructure the language, and with it the thoughts, that patients use to evaluate what they are going through so as to free them to look at things differently. In particular, I try to minimize the evaluative quality of the terms in which they regard themselves.

"I should be getting more work done, but I can't," I was told by a forty-year-old woman who had gone back to school to complete her college work.

"It would be nice if you could, but why do you use the word should? All that does is prevent you from thinking of constructive ways to improve your study habits and concentration. Why not say you'd like to find ways to do that, without passing judgment on yourself?"

I recall the wife of a friend of mine who had completely thwarted any attempts she made to communicate effectively with her husband or her only son.

"They don't tell me the truth," she repeatedly complained. "They're . . .liars." She often called them liars to their face. The word had become so stuck in her mind that she could not think of any way to improve her ability to express herself to them. Of course, they in turn would automatically become defensive whenever she brought up a subject, knowing that sooner or later, the word *liar* would be introduced into the conversation.

I knew her well enough to make a gentle suggestion, choosing my time and place with great discretion.

"Why not use the word *distort,* if you feel the need to use any word like that at all. At least you can then begin to ask yourself whether they really do distort and, if so, why. It has a better ring to it. Besides, it opens the door for discovering what the problem to be solved may really be."

The word—and the concept—*liar* vanished from her vocabulary and her mind. Instead of approaching her family as adversaries, she had set the stage for discussion.

Acquiring Information

Rebecca Holt's great disadvantage was her lack of perspective. It was obviously not her fault. At fourteen, she had neither the knowledge nor the experience to understand what was happening. Nor was she able to counteract the negative influences of the hospital environment in which she so unexpectedly found herself.

The disservice that such a lack of necessary data represents is not restricted to the young. Many of us, having led narrow and sheltered lives, have limited our range of life experience so greatly that when an unexpected turn of events occurs and we must deal with stress creatively, we are quite unprepared to do so.

Everyone who has studied creativity insists that one of the first principles in enhancing the probability of creative thought and action is to increase the amount and diversity of information and experience available to us. In this age of technology and specialization, some of us lack sufficient exposure to a wide variety of input; this is particularly true for professionals, such as scientists, physicians, engineers, and experts in every field. The problem has been complicated by the amount of study that seems to be required to become competent in any particular arena, from marketing to finance to computer program design. We are hampered even more by the abandonment of required subjects that once constituted the core curriculum in most liberal arts colleges: English, history, languages, the classics, and philosophy. While it is true that television has broadened our contact with a wide variety of issues and experiences—you can visit Africa one evening and the North Pole the next—we must keep in mind that such exposure is largely vicarious. It is not the "real thing" and cannot substitute for reality.

However, simply being exposed to new information and experience is not sufficient. Our attitude while obtaining data is as important as the nature and quality of the data we seek. There are three pairs of contrasting attitudes that we may take toward any new information. We may pursue it actively or receive it passively. We can look for differences between what we are viewing and what we have known from the past, or we can look for similarities only. We may be nonevaluative in our stance or judgmental.

The most effective approach is one that combines activity with differentiation in a nonevaluative mode. In being active, we actually look at and listen to what is around us. We do so with a searching, curious frame of mind. I kept these guidelines in mind last winter, as I walked the beach at Rendezvous Bay on Anguilla, a coral island in the Caribbean. Each time I walked the beach, I saw something new and unfamiliar, and found myself reaching strange new realizations, asking myself strange questions. For instance, one day someone brought a conch shell out of the water with the conch still in it. If you touched the creature with the tip of your finger, there would be a momentary pause, after which it would quickly draw itself deeper inside its shell. The shell itself was particularly beautiful, striped with brown and ivory. I'd seen shells like this before. But now, for the first time, I gave serious thought to the fact that this living organism had built the shell itself. Shells weren't just lying around on the ocean floor for conches to find and live in. How amazing, I considered, all these creatures, each dictated by nature to create a home for itself, each shell the same, yet each uniquely different.

I made an effort to look for differences and not just similarities. I'd walked many beaches over the years. I'd been to many tropical islands, but most of them were lusher, well endowed with rain forests and water. Coral islands are singularly parched. What grows there must struggle for life. I saw stark, contorted vegetation of a kind I had never seen before, beautiful in its simplicity, growing from small patches of fertile ground among the hills of sand.

I tried, although it was not easy, to be nonevaluative. I could not help insisting that my swimmer friend put the conch back into the sea, from which it had been so rudely taken. In my enthusiasm for the flora, I had to resist the temptation to think it was more beautiful than the rich colors of Tobago or Grenada; it was neither more beautiful nor less, only different.

My island experience may seem, on the surface, far removed from the development of creative skills to use in the service of resilience when confronted with stress. However, it was not at all. The facility that I intentionally worked to develop on Anguilla (and elsewhere) is a highly transferable skill.

Redefining the Problem

Very often the problem we are trying to solve defies solution until we restructure it by asking a different set of questions. For example, instead of trying to figure out how you and your business partners can stop arguing so much, you might restate the question and inquire how you might find new and better ways to collaborate. A high school teacher, instead of wondering why one of her pupils with a very uneven academic record is having such a hard time mastering history, might wonder why he is actually doing quite well in math and science; the answer might lead her to identify skills and motivations that could be brought to bear on the subject with which he is having trouble.

My own formulation of the concept of resilience resulted partially as a result of my efforts to redefine the problem of depression. I began to reconsider the nature of depression as it became obvious to me that being depressed per se was not an illness but a common and necessary human condition under certain stressful circumstances. If, then, being depressed was not the problem, what was? Two answers occurred to me: the failure to become depressed when we ought to, and extreme difficulty in recovering spontaneously and in a reasonable period of time from the distressing mood. Thus, the stage was set for considering the law of disruption and reintegration and the pivotal role of resilience.

Scientific research is replete with examples of breakthroughs in knowledge that have taken place once the problem under scrutiny has been repositioned. For example, Hans Selye once described to me how he arrived at his concept of stress while attending his first medical school lecture in internal medicine. The professor spoke of approaches to the examination of patients. The patients used for the demonstration all suffered with one or another infectious disease. Each of them felt and looked ill, complaining of diffuse aches and pains in the joints, intestinal disturbances, and loss of appetite; most had fever, sometimes with mental confusion. As Selye related it, the professor then moved on to itemize the specific, characteristic symptoms that permitted the diagnosis of a specific illness in each case—be it scarlet fever, measles, or influenza. But Selye's mind was somewhere else. What impressed him was the observation that most of the symptoms seemed to be common to all the patients, an idea that he later termed the "syndrome of just being sick."

By looking at these patients with the fresh, unbiased, and, in his own case, imaginative mind of a student first encountering clinical situations, he spontaneously redefined the problems in front of him by asking a question that was different from the questions the professor was encouraging him to ask. The answer to his inquiry came in his definition of stress as "the stereotyped part of the body's response to any demand, associated with the rate of wear and tear on the human machinery that accompanies any vital activity and parallels the intensity of life."

We can apply the same strategy to the issues of everyday coping. Here are several common examples:

Redefining your marital relationship: "Why do my husband (or wife) and I constantly argue?" can be turned around to ask: "How might we get along better?" You may have been asking yourself the first question for months, or even years, and never getting beyond the obvious issues that serve as the content of your arguments—money, sex, in-laws. The second, redefined question sets the stage for an entirely different list of answers, such as how you might demonstrate more generosity and thoughtfulness toward each other, or what kinds of new activities you might start to do together.

Redefining your work situation: "My job demands twelve hours a day. Add two hours of commuting time, and you can see that I haven't any left over for my family. My wife works too. How can we have any kind of home life under these circumstances?" This dilemma can be restated in new questions, as follows: "Why am I working so hard? What are my real ambitions in life? Are there other companies I can work for that would provide me with more reasonable working conditions, yet permit me to reach my career goals? Should I work in this field at all? Perhaps my wife should become the primary breadwinner."

Redefining your business operations: "The landlord is jumping the rent on our office space by two hundred percent. Where can we find the cash flow to meet this radical cost increase?" With this inquiry, you may go around in circles trying to figure out how to make more money. But if you redefine the problem, your imagination can go to work along entirely different lines. "Maybe we can get by with less space. Or, do we really need to be at this location? What parts of our business are really profitable, and what parts have been causing us to maintain our overhead at a high level while producing revenues that will just about cover it?"

Redefinition at the heart of psychotherapy: The redefinition of problems constitutes one of the prime strategies involved in psychotherapy. Therapy is often a series of reconsiderations of fundamental premises the patient has been operating on for years without being genuinely aware of their bases or impact.

Julia Blair was a forty-three-year-old woman who had become very depressed during a series of medical tests that had proved negative. An energetic, athletic person, she had not seen a physician since her last child had been born thirteen years earlier. Her girlfriends often chided her for not going at least to her gynecologist for Pap smears. "I will," she'd say, but she never did. When she missed two of her menstrual periods, which had been very regular, and then began to have profuse bleeding, she became frightened. With considerable embarrassment, she made an appointment with her doctor. For the several nights before her visit, she lay awake for hours, anxious, angry with herself, worried that she might have some form of cancer. She was obsessed by thoughts of a friend who had died of cancer the previous year; she had been only thirty-four.

The tests were unremarkable. Her physician could offer no particular explanation for her condition. After the routine dilatation and curettage procedure, during which he took the routine biopsy, the bleeding stopped, and six weeks later her menstrual periods resumed their normal rhythm. But Julia could not shake herself free of her fear.

"I can't get rid of this feeling that he missed something," she said to me. "Do you think I should see another doctor and be examined again?" We agreed that in her case, this would not be necessary or even desirable.

On the surface, the initial question was "Why was this woman so upset by a series of medical examinations that confirmed that she was in good health?" When the issue was redefined, another series of questions arose. "Why could she not accept the opinion of the doctor who had examined her?" "Had the stress of what she had been through triggered another set of emotional problems hidden from view?"

A systematic review of her past and present life revealed no obvious sources of difficulty. She had grown up in a middle-class family in a New York suburb, had attended public schools and a small midwestern college, where she performed well. She married her husband, an accountant, when she was twenty-three; the couple had two children, now in their teens. The marriage appeared to be a good one. They were financially secure. She worked part-time as an editorial assistant for a video duplicating company. Her mother was living; her father had died ten years before. She seemed to have experienced an appropriate degree of disruptive grief for an appropriate period of time. An older, married brother, also an accountant, was living and well in San Francisco. She admitted being slightly saddened by the fact her children were growing up. But otherwise, we could find no obvious sources of stress.

Following the dictum of redefining the problem, I then asked: "Could there be some reason why you might not be able to accept the fact that your life has gone so well?"

At first, she was puzzled by my inquiry. "Perhaps there is still something in your background you haven't thought to tell me," I suggested.

After we started down a few blind alleys, the following information emerged. When Julia was thirteen, her mother had had a third child, a little girl named Cynthia, who had died of crib death at the age of three months. The family had been shattered by this experience. "I hadn't thought of Cynthia until you started probing around," Julia confessed. She recalled that during her mother's pregnancy, she had been jealously anticipating the new child and only slightly appeased by her mother's plan to have her be Cynthia's godmother at the baby's christening. "I threw a terrible temper tantrum the day Mom came home from the hospital," she recounted. "After Cynthia died, I felt awfully guilty. I never spoke to anyone about how I felt. In fact, there was a family rule never to mention Cynthia. Mom kept a photo of her on her dresser, but that was the only reminder. I used to daydream about her growing up, our being friends, me being the older sister, as if she were still alive. Then that went away too."

Suddenly, Julia stopped talking and began to sob intensely, confirming the importance of what she had been recounting.

We had redefined the problem. By asking whether there might be some reason why she was having difficulty accepting what seemed like a very satisfactory life structure, we had uncovered the unresolved guilt Julia had harbored over an event that had taken place thirty years earlier. Unfinished business from the time in her life when she was entering adolescence had returned to haunt her when she reached the major bifurcation point of impending middle age. The potential threat to her own life posed by her medical condition had activated an episode of emotional disruption. Her reintegration had been obstructed by the power of the imprint of Cynthia within her unconscious and the consequent irrational feeling—that she could only now acknowledge—that she did not deserve to live and be happy herself.

Accessing the Unconscious

Dreams constitute one way to reach down into the unconscious and enlist its aid in search of creative ideas. I have always envied the chemist Kekulé, whose dream of snakes whirling about showed him the pathway to the discovery of the benzene ring. Over the years, I cannot say that I have personally had the solution to knotty problems come to me through dreams. I've had recurring dreams, such as one in which I keep searching for a particular room in a particular house. That dream disappeared some years ago, when a variety of unsettled issues in my life cleared up after an important bifurcation had passed. In the final occurrence of the dream I found the room, although I cannot describe it to this day.

When we are awake, our brain activity, as measured by the electroencephalogram, is characterized by rapid electrical waves. When we fall asleep, these are replaced by slower waves accompanied by slow, rolling, involuntary movements of our eyes, which last about ten minutes and recur every ninety minutes, so that what is called rapid-eye-movement (REM) sleep consumes about one and a half to two hours of our sleeping time each night. This is when we dream. A person is much more likely to remember a dream if awakened during REM sleep than if awakened at some other point in the sleep cycle.

Dreams have always been considered meaningful, although in different ways to different observers at different points in history. They've been viewed as prophetic, wish-fulfilling, symbolic, as a way to master some traumatic life experience. A person who has been through a severe stress, for example, such as an automobile accident, may relive it again and again in dreams until the story loses its emotional charge. Dreams may also involve subliminal perception; most of us can recall times when events that were taking place around us while we were awake, but that we were too busy or preoccupied to notice, made themselves known directly or through symbolic messages in a dream.

I have noticed a special quality about certain dreams and dreamers that suggests that dreams, beyond being clues to happenings and solutions, actually are solutions in themselves. Many of us are beset by problems in our daily lives that really originate from psychological conflicts that lie primarily within ourselves. We may find ourselves in regular conflict with friends, family, or coworkers. We may avoid spending time with our children. We may find it difficult to place our trust in others. We feel compelled to work in a frantic search for success. A period of disruption brings us to heel. We start to gain important insights into ourselves. Our behavior changes. We now get along better with others. We enjoy our youngsters. We learn to judiciously trust friends. We relax a bit from our frenetic work pace. Suddenly, the content of our dreams changes. In them, we begin to live out the conflicts or handicaps that we had previously lived in real life on a day-to-day basis. As one fifty-three-year-old woman described it: "My husband and I are getting along much better now, but at night, I've begun to dream about having the kind of awful arguments we used to have, only worse."

My friend and colleague Anthony Storr once recounted a rather ordinary, but in some ways extraordinary, discovery made through dreams, citing a story told by golfer Jack Nicklaus. After a period of some difficulty, he had suddenly regained his championship form. Nicklaus said: "I've been trying everything to find out what has been wrong. . . . Last Wednesday I had a dream . . . about my golf swing. I was hitting them pretty good in the dream, and all at once I realized I wasn't holding the club the way I've actually been holding it lately. I've been having trouble collapsing my right arm taking the club head away from the ball, but I was doing it perfectly in my sleep. So when I came to the course yesterday morning, I tried it the way I did it in my dream, and it worked."

Because of the way our mind can juxtapose perceptions and ideas and conceal them behind symbols, dreams are often not as easily deciphered as Jack Nicklaus's was. Nonetheless, the unconscious mind does work away on problems whether we're awake or asleep, and there are other ways of engaging it in our quest for creative solutions.

Simmering

Incubation is a vital part of the creative process, an important preliminary to the experience of illumination, when, often at the most unexpected moment, the answer to what we have been puzzling over for a long time suddenly flashes into consciousness. Another term for incubation is *simmering,* whereby we put aside the focus of our concerns, diverting our attention from them, so as to allow our unconscious mind to process the information and set the stage for unexpected answers.

What are we most likely to do when we are faced with a stressful situation to which we have no immediate solution? Worry about it. Go over and over it in our mind. Dwell on it. Talk about it repeatedly to the point of exasperation. Let our anxiety increase, sometimes even to the point of panic.

I'm convinced that one of the reasons for so-called interminable analysis—the situation in which the patient sees his psychotherapist week after week, month after month, year after year—is that both patient and therapist are caught up in an incessant, obsessive review of the troublesome issues that brought the patient into treatment in the first place. On the surface, it does sound logical to discuss in depth the problems associated with the patient's state of disruption. But there comes a time when going over the same ground begins to produce diminishing returns and, finally, no new results all. Not only are the forces of disruption being kept alive this way, as the therapist encourages the patient to express anger or dismay over and over again. One of the most valuable resources for the ultimate resolution of the disruption is being neglected—namely, the work that can be accomplished by the patient's preconscious mental mechanisms, which can be initiated only after concentrated attention and effort have been put aside for a time.

Interminable analysis is also a process that many of us inadvertently and unwisely carry on all by ourselves.

My first awareness of the value of simmering occurred to me in the context of searching for better ways to approach psychotherapy in patients who were suffering with depression. Realizing that repetitious discussions of disturbing material only reinforced the patients' sense of futility and hopelessness, I evolved a strategy that I called decentralization. This procedure involved distracting the patient, moving him away from his focus on depressing topics and viewpoints, and enabling him to attend to more neutral and even more positive thoughts and feelings. This may seem like common sense, but it went against all that I had been taught to practice at that time. There was no question but that depressed patients gained insight into their situations, rediscovered perspective, and recovered more quickly when decentralization was employed.

Later, when I began to understand more about the creative process, I realized that I had been applying a tactic very similar to, if not identical with, that involved in simmering. I also came to see that this was one of the most eminently practical ways to recruit the unconscious in the solution of everyday dilemmas.

How do we go about simmering? To begin with, we do everything we can do in a conscious and deliberate way to obtain all the information we can about the problem at hand. Only then, if we have not come up with solutions, should we intentionally put the problems and the information we have gathered out of our conscious mind so that our hidden mind can work on it. This is what distinguishes simmering from procrastination, which is the human frailty that tempts us to avoid thinking about or dealing with problems altogether.

Then . . . we wait. From time to time, we may go back over the issues, but usually briefly and without becoming preoccupied with them. In time—one hopes it is less rather than more—ideas will begin jumping into our mind, offering us options and perspectives we had not thought of before. One or more of these will hold the key to our perplexing situation.

"I'd been trying to figure out a way to buy or rent a house, but everything we saw was just too expensive," a thirty-two-year-old teacher told me. He and his wife had just had their third child. They were still living in a two-bedroom apartment in a development they had moved to five years earlier, when they first married. "We were driving each other nuts, living packed in that way. We must have looked at fifty properties over a two-year period. The ones we liked we couldn't afford. The ones we could afford were awful. Then my dad said to me we should just stop thinking about it for a while. Let it rest. We did. It was hard, but we did.

"Then, one morning as I woke up, it dawned on me to take out the Exxon map of the county and study it. I put my thumb on the point that showed where we lived. Then, with my little finger, I drew a circle around it. It was a shock to realize that all our efforts had been limited to the sectors north and west of our complex. I'd never thought to look south. I'd always assumed that the towns south of us were industrial. But when I looked at the map, I saw a number of small places I'd never heard of. The next Sunday we drove down to some of them. I'd been right. Half of the trip was through run-down areas and factories. But then, the space opened up again. That's how we found the place we're living in now. We love it, and we can afford it."

Successful writers know the value of simmering. You've nearly finished the draft of your manuscript. You know it's not quite right. And you don't know quite how to end the story. You can sit with a blank mind in front of your typewriter, compounding your frustration. Or you can read your material over carefully, put it aside in a desk drawer, spend a few days doing something completely unrelated to your writing. Then you return to it with freshness and enthusiasm, and, somehow, "the ending writes itself."

Great scientists know it too. This is exactly one of the tactics that permitted Louis Pasteur to discover the principle of immunization. Pasteur had been carrying out research on fowl cholera. This was interrupted by a summer vacation. When he returned to work, nearly all the germ cultures were sterile. He tried to revive the microbes by injecting them into fowl. The birds were unaffected. He was about to give up, when he had the serendipitous notion to reinoculate the fowl with a powerful fresh culture. To his surprise, nearly all these pretreated fowl remained healthy in spite of the inoculation. From this observation came the idea that exposure to infection could change the organism's system so as to render it resistant to future infection.

We can speculate that Pasteur's vacation may have been a more important contribution to his discovery than the fact that it gave the germs a chance to die and set the stage for his efforts to revive them. It may have turned his attention away from its main focus and prepared him to see what he was viewing in a new way upon his return.

Peripheral vision can be turned inward no less than toward the outer world. During the period of simmering, this radar-like scanning remains operative, ready to pick up whatever messages our hidden mind may choose to deliver. How they will be delivered—through dreams, sudden hunches, or inspirations that jump into consciousness while we are walking a country lane on a brisk autumn day—will vary from person to person and from message to message. The important thing is for us to understand the process. Like everything else about creative thinking, the more we practice it, the more proficient we will become.

1 6

More Creative Tactics

Distancing

Erika Marchand had had a child out of wedlock when she was twenty-four. Five years later, she was still living at home with her parents.

"I don't really know why I came to see you," she said during our first visit. "I certainly haven't had a nervous breakdown. You might call it quiet desperation, but then that's the kind of life I assume most people live, even if they won't admit it . . . except for those times when the desperation gets pretty loud."

Erika's father was seventy years old, a retired executive who had bailed out with a handsome parachute when the company of which he had been executive vice president was taken over by a well-known corporate raider. Her mother, in her middle sixties, was a handsome, elegant woman, accustomed over the years to entertaining her husband's prestigious acquaintances. This was an activity that had ceased abruptly when he was no longer visible in the boardroom. She had also given freely of her time and energy to a wide variety of community charities. They had lived most of their lives in a suburb of New York, but for the past seven years, having sold their home, they had lived in a three-bedroom ranch house that had been their summer home in Osterville, Massachusetts, on Cape Cod.

Erika had two sisters. One was thirty-two, married to a lawyer, and living ten minutes from her parents' home. The other, twenty-six, worked in a gift shop in Hyannis and maintained her own apartment there. On the surface, the family seemed as if they enjoyed, for this day and age, a singular and perhaps admirable degree of closeness and cohesion.

"I've never had my own place," Erika said. "I moved in with my parents after college. I did work on my master's degree in history for a year. I commuted to classes, and never finished. Then I had the baby. For the past couple of years I've been working part-time for a decorator in town, just trying to get my act together. I've thought of leaving . . . going to California, or maybe even further. But I seem to suffer with this . . ." She struggled to find the right word. "Inertia."

What emerged was the picture of a family that could not tolerate change. "Every time I went away to college, Mom would act like I was going to the North Pole. My younger sister was nearly married twice; they were nice guys, but Mom did nothing but pick them apart until my sister broke up with them. When my older sister's husband was offered a good position in Washington, you'd have thought Mom was going to have a convulsion, she carried on so. So they stayed put."

I asked her about her father. "He doesn't get involved," Erika said.

Whatever other problems Erika might have had, it was apparent to me that a powerful force was operative within her family structure that pulled everything to the center. In both obvious and subtle ways, her mother—with her father's full collaboration—thwarted the efforts of all the children to grow up and leave home, psychologically as well as geographically.

"How did your family react to the baby?" I asked.

"Not at all the way I'd expected. I thought they'd be furious, scream or yell or something, tell me to leave home. Instead, it was as if nothing special had happened. I suppose that was good in a way. Mom helped me through the pregnancy. When I came home, you'd have thought it was their baby instead of mine. Eerie."

"How does your family handle conflicts?" I asked. "I mean, specifically, do they argue or disagree and get things resolved by talking about them?"

"Are you kidding?" Erika asked. "You don't disagree with Mom or Dad about anything, unless you want her to sulk at the dinner table and him to stop talking for the rest of the evening."

She thought for a moment. "I was furious a couple of months ago," she said. "I'd been thinking of moving out, maybe going away to Boston or even San Francisco now that my little girl is old enough for preschool. I'd gone to a woman in town who does word processing and got her to put together a résumé. I was going to send it to a bunch of places. Retail sales training programs. I thought I'd be good at retailing. I gave them to Dad and asked him to mail them for me. I even stamped them. A week later I found them stacked up on his desk in his study. I blew my top. He looked perplexed and said he had forgotten. Mom heard me. She came into the room and told me not to talk to my father that way and that if I had wanted them mailed, I should have mailed them myself. So I picked them up and walked out to the kitchen and tore them up and threw them into the trash can."

"Why didn't you mail them?" I asked.

"If I knew the answer to that," she said, "I wouldn't be here talking to you now."

It required little imagination to see that Erika and, undoubtedly, her sisters as well were prisoners of a family homeostasis that was rigid, unyielding, resistant to change, and continually obstructing the natural evolution of personal space and self-determination. Moreover, I could safely assume that this problem had become incorporated into Erika's personality itself so that, on the whole, she no longer required her parents' reactions to keep her within the confines of home. Her own behavior would serve that end without the need for any further cues from them. I realized that we had two jobs to carry out: giving Erika more freedom within herself to define her life, and enabling her to separate herself from the actual environmental conditions that had fostered and preserved her helplessness.

She needed to distance herself, internally as well as externally.

Knowing how resistant people such as Erika can be to this objective, I realized that we would have to accomplish it slowly, a step at a time. Even though she could easily have done so, she had not left the Cape in two years, except for an occasional day trip to Boston or New York. I suggested that she take a vacation, time away from the situation, but something with meaning—Europe, perhaps.

Predictably, her parents expressed their skepticism about this advice. Her mother made numerous innuendos about the dangers of international traveling with the hostage situation being what it was. Her father wondered why she bothered to spend his money and her time going all the way to New York to see a psychiatrist if that was the best advice such an expert could provide.

Nonetheless, Erika went. When she returned, she seemed more enthusiastic about life. Of course, she had only been given a temporary boost, a taste of what she could do and what she could feel like freed of stagnation. Inner, psychological changes would have to be made too.

"You might begin by dressing differently," I said. Erika had worn blue jeans and a wrinkled blouse each time she had come for her appointment. When I suggested she buy some dresses and perhaps even a couple of sporty outfits, she balked at first, until I explained to her that the simple procedure of changing the way you dress can activate change by shifting self-image. She agreed to try.

But, of course, at the core of Erika's difficulties was the fact that she had no idea of what she wanted to become, not even how or where she wanted to bring up her little girl. She had forgotten how to dream. Sitting on the yellow corduroy couch in my office, she slowly listed all the options she had considered over the years, from retailing, her most recent idea, to archaeology, an ambition that she had entertained in college and had been part of her motivation to try to earn her master's degree in history years before. She recounted them with a curious indifference.

"All right, now," I said. "Let's play a game. Move to that chair." I pointed to a black wooden captain's chair that stood in front of my desk. She obliged me, smiling self-consciously.

"Look at the couch, where you were sitting. Pretend that you and I are colleagues and we're here to talk with each other about why Erika Marchand is having so much difficulty trying to figure out what to do with her life."

"This is absurd," she remarked.

"Of course it is, but try it anyway."

"Well, Erika," she began, "you've got so many talents you don't know which one to use. We live in a world that forces everyone to specialize, and you don't want to specialize because that means giving up a lot of things that interest you. It means giving up freedom, which is why you didn't marry Sam when he wanted to marry you and why you can't decide whether you ever want to get married to anyone."

I urged her to continue.

"How can you think about getting on with your life and being a mother when you can't even bring yourself to leave home?"

I detected a note of anger in her voice and called it to her attention. Then I suggested she go back and sit on the couch and reply to herself.

No sooner had she reseated herself than she began to cry. "If I go away," she said, "my parents will get old and die . . . and I'll get old too."

"Are you suggesting that by doing nothing, you can make time stand still?"

She looked amazed. "When I was a little kid, I wanted that kind of power . . . to make time stop. How could you know that? I haven't thought of that in years."

"I didn't need a crystal ball to figure that out. It was obvious in what you just told me. Now, let's try again. Tell me, quickly, all the things you've thought of doing with your life and let's add a few more, whatever might occur right now."

She reviewed her list of ambitions and added to them, but this time much more quickly and with excitement in her voice. What I had accomplished—by the simple maneuver of having her change her location and her role in our session for a few minutes—was to put distance between her obsolete set of conditioned responses and a new Erika, albeit a slightly fictitious one. The floodgates of her imagination opened, joining me in a mutual effort toward self-determination.

Over the months, as we continued our work, she concluded that she wanted to move to Boston and finish her studies. "It's not exactly the most practical thing to do, but it's what I want, and it will give me time to get my bearings over the next year. I'll have a chance to meet new friends, maybe even someone special. And I'll have time to be a mother too."

Erika's mother sulked for hours on the day of her departure. Her father gave her a weak handshake instead of a hug, reassuring her that if things didn't work out, she could always come home to live again. They even offered to keep their grandchild with them, suggesting that they could bring her up much better than their daughter could, an offer Erika politely refused. She saw no point in trying to explain to them the changes that had taken place in her attitudes and behavior. The last time I heard from Erika, she wrote me that she had met a man with whom she had fallen in love, and that she had been accepted in a training program with an international auction house that would give her the freedom to live and work practically anywhere in the world. Once a month she traveled home with her little girl to visit her parents. She had learned to recognize many of their maneuvers to control her, and even the child, or to discourage her enterprise; she dismissed these without the guilty and immobilized responses she had previously experienced. Interestingly, she informed me that her married sister and her husband had also moved away, to Washington. "Maybe," she wrote, "they were inspired by my example."

I've selected Erika's case because it illustrates how important distancing is as a technique to deal with problems that need creative solutions. Putting space between you and your problems can be an invaluable way to relieve the pressure they're producing, give you new perspectives on what you're trying to work out, and afford you the opportunity both to simmer—thus tapping unconscious resources—and to think more freely and clearly of new options.

Distancing can give us important clues to sources of stress when we're not sure what these sources may be. Consider the potential impact leaving and subsequently reentering a stressful situation can have. We often become so accustomed or attuned to stress that we may become aware of its presence and effects on us only by removing ourselves from it for a time and then returning to the scene of our problems.

I recall a close friend of mine approaching his sixty-first birthday. He was a physician, employed as assistant medical director of a suburban community hospital. He'd been suffering with insomnia, nervousness, and low spirits for several months until he took his annual vacation. He and his wife flew to Paris, where they rented a car and drove through the Loire Valley, then on to Provence, finally flying back from Marseilles to Paris and thence home again. During the entire trip, he felt exhilarated. However, within a few days after his return, he felt exhausted again. He was again unable to fall asleep for hours at night. Why would returning home reactivate his distress, he asked himself. He discovered the answer by giving serious thought to the nature of his work. It seemed that his hospital was being affected by new rules set up to control third-party payments for patient care; rather than reimbursing the hospital for treatment given, as had been the policy in the past, the authorities allotted a certain amount of money to the care of patients entirely on the basis of a schedule of costs determined by the patients' diagnoses. For example, a heart attack was defined as treatable in a predetermined amount of time, and a limited amount of reimbursement was allowed to pay these costs.

He believed he had come to terms with these policies. "I know this is an attempt to control skyrocketing costs," he said to me once over lunch, "and that if hospitals had policed themselves better, it might not have come to this. But, still, I don't feel as free or responsible as I used to feel. I honestly believe my treatment of patients is often compromised by these bureaucratic restrictions."

Six months later, he attended a cardiology convention in Australia that lasted a week. On his return, he telephoned me from Kennedy International Airport as soon as he had cleared customs. "I'm in a state of panic," he said. "I've got to talk with you right away." It was nearly 8:00 P.M. I told him to come directly to my home.

He was no longer able to deny the obvious. Clearly, his working situation was causing him intense stress. Except for his troublesome symptoms, he had been able to ignore this fact on a day-to-day basis, becoming more or less acclimated to his environment. However, when he distanced himself from his ordinary surroundings for a while and then returned to them, the impact of the stress-inducing situation grew in its intensity.

Reluctantly, he concluded that he found it impossible to continue work that violated his personal ethical principles. "Other people have learned to do it. I thought I had too, but I just can't do it anymore."

Through a medical placement bureau, he was able to locate a job, working as a partner in a private-practice group. His spirits improved almost as soon as he had decided to make a change, and during the first year on his new job, he continued to feel well and in renewed command of his professional activities.

What distancing can accomplish is to loosen up our minds and free us from our natural inclination to home in on problems so intensely that we defeat our efforts to resolve them. Consider an argument between a husband and wife. It is not their first, and it is not their first about money. It's nine-thirty in the evening on April fifteenth. Their accountant has just delivered the income tax returns. He urges her to sign them so he can promptly get them into the mail. She refuses, insisting that as she is responsible for what's in them no less than he is, she wants to read them carefully first. Her eye catches a series of losses on the page where stock transactions are noted. Angrily, she asks him whether he has been gambling with commodity options again. He raises his voice, protesting it's his money and his right to do so. She reminds him it's "their" money. He tries to press a pen into her hand and demands she sign. In tears, she throws the return on the floor and stalks into the bedroom. He follows her. After two hours of mutual castigation, realizing that it is half past eleven, she reluctantly acquiesces so that the envelope can be dropped at the post office before midnight. The taxes have been filed, but the argument continues, at breakfast the next morning, at dinner the next evening, and the evening after that. Finally, words like *divorce* creep into the turmoil, and the couple appear no closer to resolving the impasse between her sense of outrage at his disrespect for her rights and opinions and his stubborn adherence to his wish to speculate with money "he has earned."

How might distancing have helped such a controversy?

That her angry reaction was justified is probably indisputable. They were not wealthy; the money lost could well have been put to better purposes. That his speculating in commodities, although risky, might lead to considerable financial gain is also true. Properly managed, the disruption in their relationship triggered by the information on the income tax return could have set the stage for improved and shared management of their money and a better relationship overall. But as long as they were caught up in adversarial stances, focusing day after day on hurt feelings and personal affronts, they could not proceed to an analysis or understanding of the real issues involved. For example, why did he not discuss investment decisions with her beforehand? Does he question her judgment? Is he simply arbitrary? Is he basically insecure and afraid of having his ego compromised? Has this kind of problem recurred throughout their marriage? Has she exaggerated the amount and seriousness of the loss? Was he caught off guard in a moment of weakness by an acquaintance in the brokerage business and too embarrassed to tell her what had happened when the losses occurred? Has she overreacted because her own father, years before, had lost the family fortune in oil futures?

If, after the initial explosion, they had agreed to take a breather—distancing themselves from the heat of their argument for a day or so—they might have been able to return to the issue with clear minds and more calmly explore what was involved. Such a discussion, in turn, might well have provided the ground-work for resolution.

Modern psychology has told us that we all suffer with a tendency to run away from problems rather than face and deal with them. There's much truth in that. However, we have also come to underestimate the enormous value that a vacation from troubles can serve—literally, by taking the family on a trip to Disneyland or taking walks in the woods on sunny days all by ourselves, or figuratively, by temporarily tabling issues (with others, or within our own minds) to which there are no obvious, immediate solutions.

Play

Play contributes substantially to creative behavior. If we take a closer look at what play is, we see that it represents a specific form of what psychologists call cognitive dissonance, the ability to operate on more than one level of thought at a time and to entertain seemingly contradictory ideas more or less comfortably. We are free; yet we are guided by rules. We are spontaneous; yet we operate within a ritual. The freedom makes it playful. The rules and rituals make it nonthreatening by keeping it contained.

Playing hide and seek, Monopoly, Clue. Dressing up in costume. Racing toy cars. Furnishing dollhouses. Building model airplanes. Joining Little League. The list is too long and too obvious to require further elaboration. What is important to acknowledge is that the play we engage in, as children and, in precious moments, as adults, is spontaneous and essentially safe. This makes it a marvelous testing ground for new ideas.

I've always enjoyed a description of play given me by a colleague, psychiatrist Peter Hogan. "A progression of play typical of Americans," he noted, "begins with the peekaboo game of the infant, in which nothing is at stake; proceeds through the games of childhood, where the children go home secure in the knowledge that no matter what has happened at play, the most important part of their lives—their family—has not changed; and goes on to high school and college athletics, where prestige outside the stadium, girls, status, sometimes jobs are at stake, and the players are far from playful. Where there is much at stake and where the player is aware that there is much at stake, the game becomes very serious indeed. Imagine the infant in peekaboo not knowing whether or not his mother will really return!"

Play is a critical form of learning. When the infant plays the peekaboo game, he grasps something about being separate from his mother; he learns to rely on her reliability. He is not afraid, because he is sure she will return, and her return is, itself, a source of excitement and fulfillment. When the older child learns how to play with other children, he acquires a wide range of verbal and nonverbal communication skills, without which his world, his place within it, and his interactions with it will remain unpredictable and erratic.

Many of us, as we grow older, become so serious about our pastimes that we eliminate the fun they could provide us. We engage in games with such focus and intensity that they no longer provide us with the creative exuberance we felt as children. Some even eliminate play from their lives altogether. This is an unfortunate loss, and a potentially dangerous one.

As Anthony Storr once pointed out: "Human beings are creatures of opportunity. Our responses are variable, not fixed, and we must remain alert in order to recognize opportunity when it comes. Play keeps us from falling into a torpor we can ill afford."

How else does play serve the interests of creativity and resilience? To begin with, it is a form of diversion; as such, it represents another way to distance ourselves in the pursuit of survival and solutions. It is a valuable way to reduce tension. Under conditions of stress, muscular tension increases; this is part of the body's readiness to deal with conflict and happens even when such conflict is of a psychological or social nature. Athletic activities, from briskly walking to playing tennis, offer us an opportunity to relax and restore our muscles to their prestress level of equilibrium.

For some of us caught in drab jobs, lonely lives, or unrewarding marriages, an afternoon on the golf course, a tennis game on brightly lit indoor courts, sailing, and innumerable other pastimes may provide us with our own special meaning in life: the chance to master a skill and to use our minds and bodies in exciting harmony. For many a soldier waiting for months for the moment of battle, card games undoubtedly relieved the awful monotony and helped distract him from his fear.

There is one more connection between play and creativity. It is a source of delight, an experience that loosens the constrictions of the mind as surely as exercise loosens the tautness of the body. Such enthusiasm encourages spontaneity and catalyzes the emergence of new insights along with a host of such positive emotions as love, hope, and the will to do.

Humor

Laughter is a marvelous form of distancing. Because humor involves absurdities, it also can promote new and unusual thought patterns. Moreover, it promotes a radical, swift change in our perception of a situation or event, even if only momentarily. Such altered perceptions can alert us to the fact that a new set of circumstances exists and that we must respond appropriately to this change. Thus the temptation to deny the reality of change may be mitigated, because we will probably feel less threatened by its potential seriousness as well as its possibly enduring nature.

I use humor often in the context of my work, being most attentive to the importance of timing and careful not to use it unkindly at my patients' or my own expense. I recall, for example, a somewhat hypochondriacal woman in her early forties who was afraid that she might develop every new disease that she read about in *Vogue* magazine. Although her own physician had repeatedly reassured her that she was in good health, he consistently did so in a very serious and professional manner, mingled with frustration when he sensed that his efforts were of little avail. After I had come to know her well and she had learned to feel confident and secure in our relationship. I realized that if she was to relinquish to some degree her preoccupation with health, I would have to use tactics that would catch her off guard and enable her to see how unrealistic her worries were.

One day, having read an article about Alzheimer's disease, she came to see me complaining that her memory was failing her. "I've lost my fountain pen," she said, "and my appointment book. I even left my umbrella in the taxi on the way here. I must be losing my mind." I reassured her that while she might be preoccupied and consequently not paying due attention to things, she had none of the signs or symptoms of Alzheimer's. She reacted to my comments with seeming indifference, sitting tense and straight at the edge of her chair. Seeing no visible relief, I realized that a different approach to reassurance—one that might compel her into reconsidering her attitude—was in order.

She gave me the opportunity when she asked me to read a letter she had written to her former husband asking him to be more timely in the payment of child support. "Can I borrow your reading glasses?" I asked. "I've misplaced mine." It happened to be true.

She instantly burst into laughter and asked: "What did you ask me for?"

"I don't recall. What did I ask you for?"

She shifted to a more relaxed position and sat there with a knowing smile. There was no need to discuss the matter any further at that moment, so, borrowing her glasses, I read the note she handed me.

Another example of the insight-producing power of humor involves an exchange I had with a close friend of mine, a professional colleague in his mid-fifties, with whom I have often had lengthy discussions about our lives and our work. We have a number of acquaintances in common. Of one of these, my friend once told me how he had tried to reach him again and again on the phone but had never received a return call.

"He infuriates me by his rudeness," my friend said.

"You have to understand his situation," I replied. "Maybe he's under a lot of pressure. You know what he's been going through lately. You shouldn't feel so angry about this."

"I know his situation. I can feel sorry for him. But I'm mad nonetheless." Then he said: "You shouldn't tell me what I'm supposed to feel. That's like adding injury to insight."

His clever play on the common phrase "don't add insult to injury" made me laugh. I quickly realized that I had developed a bad habit of telling him what I thought he should or should not feel. He was protesting, through humor, making it clear to me that what he felt was what he felt, justified or not. I got the point and immediately began watching for that tendency in our conversations.

Beyond insight, the emotional release that humor provides must have tension-reducing and health-promoting qualities in its own right. The complex psychobiological nature of humor and its effect on hormones, immune systems, and the like has really never been adequately explored, but author and editor Norman Cousins has presented a convincing case for the role that humor may have played in his recovery from illness. Lying in his hospital bed, Cousins watched a series of comedy films, such as Marx Brothers movies, believing that laughter itself would afford him a curative power that doctors, nurses, and medications could never effect by themselves.

It never ceases to surprise me that innumerable books about stress and its management omit the topic of humor entirely. Either the experts are too serious about their subject or they have failed to appreciate the central role that humor plays in our adaptation to change and, especially, in how we view ourselves.

In the classic film *Singing in the Rain*—which I have seen a dozen times and which always leaves me feeling better—Donald O'Connor sings and dances to a melody whose lyrics seem unforgettably pertinent: "Make them laugh, make them laugh . . ." When laughter comes, can hope be far behind?

PART IV

Resilience in the World Around Us

17

The World Around Us

L IVING BEINGS are open systems in continuing contact with each other, yet separate from everything else in the universe. Physically speaking, this demarcation corresponds to the skin surface of our bodies. Psychologically, it is invisible, encompassing all that happens within our minds—ideas, feelings, dreams, hopes. At one and the same time, it is our protection from and our access to what lies beyond us. Through our senses—sight, hearing, touch, taste, smell—we detect information. This information is then transmitted to our brains for interpretation and understanding. By gesture and articulation, we communicate with the outside world, conveying concepts and responses created within ourselves either as a reaction to sensory provocation or as a self-generated product of our own minds.

Even though I'd been raised with due attention paid to the importance of the quality of the people around me in the development of character, I must confess that during my formative years in psychiatry, I succumbed to the charm and excitement of psychoanalysis no less than many of my colleagues did; there, the focus was almost exclusively on the inner workings of the individual mind. The idea that the people who surrounded patients might make or break their recovery or that the conditions under which patients lived and worked might significantly alter the course of their illness and recovery seemed curiously irrelevant.

I shall always recall the situation in which I first came to appreciate the futility of the purely intrapsychic psychoanalytic vision. I'd been carrying out therapy with a thirty-two-year-old management consultant who was depressed. Bob Morris was the youngest partner in a middle-sized firm in Manhattan. Having graduated with honors from the University of Chicago Business School, he had been offered a number of excellent starting positions. He selected the one he thought most opportune. With his twelve-hour workdays, grueling attention to endless details, weeks abroad in Europe evaluating the operations of American corporations, sleepless nights at printers checking each word and phrase in foot-thick reports, he consistently won the respect and admiration of his clients and colleagues.

In one sense, Bob's depression was a form of battle fatigue. From a more strictly psychoanalytic viewpoint, it had been activated by the death of his father, who, in Bob's eyes, had been a complete failure. An alcoholic, Gus Morris had been unemployed most of his life. He was given to beating Bob's mother from time to time. He totally ignored his bright, competent son. Bob was determined to outdo him, and he did so, easily. But Bob's guilt over his hostility toward this man had brought him to his knees.

I prescribed antidepressants. Within a few weeks, Bob felt quite a bit better. However, in spite of his outstanding record of accomplishment, his self-esteem continued to be poor. "I feel I haven't done anything worthwhile with my life," he'd repeat. "My success has always been due to luck."

One of his primary complaints involved his relationships with people. "Except for work, I avoid them," he said. "I'd rather be by myself reading than waste my time in idle dinner-table talk." It had not always been that way for Bob. At college, he had been active in student government and taken part in theatrical productions; for one year, he had served as president of his fraternity. "You could say that this . . . withdrawal . . . started after I married," he observed.

Months went by. Bob seemed to have reached a plateau in his recovery. He was no longer depressed, to be sure, but he felt "empty," "directionless," "like giving everything up and going somewhere to drop out of sight." I began to wonder if I were missing something.

Then, after careful thought, I chose to violate one of the cardinal rules of psychoanalysis as it was then practiced. I asked to meet Bob's wife, Betsy.

At first, she refused to come. Then, once he had made clear to her that the purpose of the visit was only to obtain information about him that might help in his treatment, she agreed. Twice she canceled her appointment at the last minute. The third time, she kept it, arriving twenty minutes late.

"I'm here for Bob's sake," she immediately reminded me. I was surprised by her appearance. From Bob's description, I had expected a more soft-spoken, articulate, warm, and insightful woman. Instead, she spoke in a high-pitched, strident voice, responding somewhat curtly to my questions and offering little spontaneously.

Bob and Betsy had met as undergraduates. They were married during his second year at business school. "He studied all the time. We hardly did anything together. Of course, I didn't know then that he had mental problems," she told me, betraying a feeling that Bob should be forever indebted to her for marrying him. "He's been lucky," she said, making no effort to hide her opinion that Bob's success was more a matter of timing than of enterprise. "I assume he told you that his making partner was due to the fact I cultivated a friendship with the senior partner's wife."

Her criticism of Bob poured out. "He doesn't give anything to anybody. He's selfish. We had a good sex life in the early years, but he hasn't been interested for years. If he were more of a man, I'd suspect him of having an affair. But not Bob!"

When I told her our time was nearly up and expressed my thanks for her help, she ended the visit with a pointed question.

"How long is this pampering going to go on, Doctor?"

After Betsy had left, I felt a premonition of hopelessness. The woman Bob had described to me and the one I had just met were totally different. He had emphasized her supportiveness. During her visit with me, her contempt for Bob had permeated the session. Could I bring him to see the discrepancies? Should I? Could he go on living with her if he understood the demoralizing influence she represented in his life?

Was he, indeed, innocent? Or had he, through selfishness and lack of consideration, subtly collaborated with her to bring out the worst in both of them? Could he gain a healthy sense of self-esteem while living within the framework of such a marriage? Could she change?

It seemed to me that all the psychoanalysis in the world would fail to make a dent in Bob's psyche as long as things at home remained the way they were.

I never had a chance to discover the answers to my questions. Prodded by Betsy's criticisms of our encounter, Bob shortly thereafter quit therapy. I heard nothing further of them until, twenty years later, I learned through friends the tragic news that one of their adolescent sons had committed suicide.

But I never forgot the lesson I had learned: Resilience is not an exclusively interior quality. Its existence, growth, and survival depend significantly on what and who fills the space around us and the nature of the balance that exists between ourselves and that outer world.

The Role of Structure

In determining whether or not an environment supports resilience, we must first consider the degree and extent of external structure itself. Here we see an intimate relationship between structure and the life cycle. During infancy, a high degree of consistent structure is essential for healthy development. The need for structure remains throughout childhood and adolescence, even though the geography of structures steadily expands beyond the front door of home to the corridors of school and the streets between, and in spite of the fact that the teenager, in his search for autonomy, bristles and takes frequent exception to the very structure that he still requires.

Perhaps most of us find ourselves with the least amount of structure during our early adult years, when we're still unmarried, uncommitted, and exploring life's dimensions. However, as soon as you fall in love with someone, you create another structure, and, if and when you marry and have children, you create an even more complex one. The difference between the structure of your original family and your new one is that the former was basically thrust upon you, while the latter represents a creation of your own. In terms of your occupation or career, you will find yourself within a framework that will be more or less defined and afford you varying degrees of freedom and opportunity.

As you approach middle age and move through it, the nature of the structures that surround you will change, but structure will be there nonetheless; and as you grow older, you will, as you did during childhood, require an increasing amount of structure to provide you with support.

One of the questions every adult should consider is just how much structure suits his or her personality. Ideally, the kind of person you are and the degree to which the world around you is structured will match. For example, if you are very independent and self-determining, you may do better in an environment that is more loosely constructed. If, on the other hand, you are someone who needs to know where you are positioned within the world and depends on outside guidelines to orient yourself and help you live your life, then you will need a world that is better defined and more coherently put together.

Most of us prefer definition and do better when the world around us is structured, and we can be quite threatened when such structure is removed. Harry Matthews, for example. Harry had been a career officer in the army. He'd served during the Second World War as an artillery captain, and had stayed on for another fifteen years, retiring when he reached forty-two. Within six months after his retirement, he became severely depressed. Harry had tried to build his own business. He and his wife had purchased a small motel along the North Carolina coast, something they had talked of and dreamed about for years. Harry's job was to handle the money, promote their enterprise, and supervise the motel's routine maintenance. Hers was to manage the housekeeping services and the operations of the coffee shop. His disruption had been triggered by their accountant's report to the effect that if things did not correct themselves, the business would be bankrupt by the end of the year.

Harry's drinking did not help. Nor did his impulsive spending on items that could have been done without, for a while at least, such as expensive brochures, a fake brick exterior, and a full-time secretary. His wife tried to restrain him, but Harry, being stubborn, egotistical, and determined, did not listen.

For twenty years of his adult life, Harry Matthews had lived and worked within a structure that had been highly organized, the United States Army. There had been a routine for practically every detail. He was told when to get up and when to go to bed, what to wear, when to call his men to muster, what forms to fill out, what inventories to order. Only within the confines of his home—and even that was on the base and maintained by the military—did he enjoy some personal freedom. Within such a highly structured world, he performed exceedingly well.

However, once the external structure had been removed and he was left to his own devices, Harry could not manage to stay organized in his behavior. He had, in fact, never had the opportunity to learn how to do so, having gone directly from the structure of school to the structure of the army. Now, in his own business, he found himself floundering and making mistakes that could threaten his solvency.

Harry spoke of his problems with the pastor of his church, who recognized that he was not about to accept a recommendation to seek out professional psychotherapy. Moreover, his problems had to be solved quickly and definitively. He recommended Alcoholics Anonymous; that would provide him with some structure. Harry took his suggestion. The pastor also recommended he attend courses in hotel management, hire a manager (an option the budget would not permit), or find out if he could affiliate with one of the large motel chains then exploding throughout the country. Harry and his wife chose the last solution. They became franchisees. Once again, although some of his newly found independence had been preserved, Harry became part of a structure that told him what to do and how to do it, restoring the control he sorely required.

Most of us depend on structure. Whether we feel more content within the context of family life or as a single among single friends, working our way up the ladder in a company or as a member of a union, we like to know where we are and where we are going, and we take our signals from the world around us. For most of us, being without structure is like being in the center of a nightmare.

Why is structure so necessary? Structure provides us with guidelines for our behavior and definitions for our hopes and expectations. We are creatures of habit. We like to know which train we have to take to work in the morning so as to arrive on time. We like to know what homework is expected the next day in school. (Whether we do it in a timely fashion or not is another issue.) We like to have an idea where we're positioned in a hierarchy of people—boss, coworker, employee. We feel more secure knowing what skills we require to do a job and being in command of them. With feigned amusement and secret fear, many people read the daily newspaper horoscopes in search of more structure and predictability than life affords.

Resilient Surroundings

Given, then, a certain quantity of structure (how much depends on our individual requirements), what qualities should such structures possess to permit us to be resilient?

To begin with, people who are understanding, loyal, accepting, empathetic, and supportive. Recent studies have shown conclusively that people recovering from serious emotional disruptions do much better if they are surrounded by a network of understanding friends and family members than if they emerge from their troubled times to be greeted by hostile, confusing, indifferent, or rejecting people, or no people at all. This sounds like common sense. However, to their credit, the scientists who have proved the obvious have, by doing so, underscored the importance of one of the characteristics of environmental structures that facilitate resilience: positive human contact.

Over the years, I have been able to identify a number of elements in our environments necessary to facilitate resilience. Not surprisingly, these mesh well with basic features of the resilient personality. They include the following:

- Coherent but flexible structures
- A human network
- Respectfulness
- Recognition
- Assurance of privacy
- Tolerance of change
- Acceptance
- Defined, realistic limits on behavior
- Open communications
- Responsiveness to new ideas
- Tolerance of a conflict
- Promotion of reconciliation
- Hopefulness
- A sense of community
- Constructive human values
- Empathy

Empathy is the ability to feel, whether from past experience or intuitively, what another human being is feeling, be it joy, sorrow, anger, fear. Many people who consult therapists do so because they are starved for empathy. Spiritual loneliness often brings them to the point of such desperation that they are forced to acknowledge their pain and reach out for help. They are searching for a depth of human contact that has been denied them previously, and perhaps eluded them everywhere else they may have sought it.

Supportive environments are those in which open communications are encouraged. Such communications should be realistic, not distorted and misleading. Few of us are immune to the impact of another person's impression of us. If friends and family have faith in us and our abilities, their confidence will reinforce our own sense of personal worth and competence. If they offer us appropriate feedback, putting into words what is wrong as well as what is right, they give us the chance to hold on to (or regain) perspective when ours is in danger of being lost.

The freedom to express what we believe and our willingness to give others the same privilege is part of an open communication system. We must be able to share ideas, hopes, dreams, disagreements. And when, in the interests of our purposes or of the relationships we value, our disagreements demand some sort of resolution, we must know how to master reconciliation as well.

"Only after I had the experience of working with several different partners did I know what the difference between a good and bad partnership really was," a twenty-eight-year-old business woman once told me. "Kathy was the first. If I disagreed with her, I knew I was going to be in for an hour's verbal dissertation on why my point of view was wrong. She wouldn't get angry or anything. She'd just lecture me, repeating herself again and again until I was exhausted. She never seemed to tire out. If I brought up some new angle, it was as if she just didn't hear me. Oh, she'd say yes and let me go on. But when I was finished, she'd return to her last comment as if I had never said a word. Now with Jerry, our ideas build on each other. If I tell her—or she tells me—that there's a disagreement, we quickly look at the issues. We don't always come around to each other's opinion, but when we don't, we admit we don't and table the issues for reconsideration at a later date. Now, that's a partnership."

A supportive environment must be responsive. A middle-aged advertising executive recently told me that he has made a policy of not answering most of his mail and not returning the majority of his phone calls. He blamed his behavior on his being inundated with work and attributed his indifference to "oversaturation." I guess the human nervous system can tolerate only a certain amount of stimulation before it gets short-circuited and turns off. But there should be a better way to handle things than that. If I should ever have reason to contact him—which I very much doubt—I would at least like the courtesy of a return phone call or a postcard, even if the message is that he is too busy to talk with me. At least, I'd know that I exist. That's called recognition. And I would feel as though I were being treated with respect.

Clearly, an environment that treats you with respect and responds, in some way, to your presence enhances resilience, even as one that ignores or actively abuses you will obstruct it. Some child and adolescent psychiatrists have described our present culture as dehumanizing. To this dehumanizing quality, they attribute a number of our social ills, from drug abuse to teenage suicide. What they are referring to goes well beyond the ordinary parameters of respect for others. They are taking a good, hard look at the underpinnings of our culture and suggesting that a serious lack of traditional human values lies at the heart of many of our problems.

I believe they're right. For among the basic elements of an environment that fosters resilience is a set of positive values to live by. What such values are is no mystery. We call them basic human rights (and responsibilities). Psychologist Carl Jung described them when he spoke of the collective unconscious—those imprints of human experience that lie buried within each and every one of us and that, from the beginning of time, have represented the essential ingredients in our personal and genetic survival and evolution. Nurturing, loyalty, justice, generosity, forgiveness, love. We know what they are, and while we may strive to practice them in our own lives, we cannot afford to disregard their importance in the structures that surround us.

Destructive environments pay little heed to Jung's archetypes. Overly rigid or extensively disorganized, they give little support to, and more commonly thwart, resilience. Some of their more obvious characteristics are listed in the following table of polarities:

DEBILITATING ENVIRONMENTAL STRUCTURES

Too Rigidly Organized	*Too Much Disarray*
Abusive or demanding	Indulgent
Excessive expectations	Murky expectations
Stubborn resistance to change	Excessively fluid
Rejecting/ambivalent	Overly permissive
Discourages communications	Indiscreet
Intolerant of conflict	Perpetuates turmoil
Punitive or vindictive	Excess forebearance
Thwarts hope	Pollyannaish
Rejects new ideas	Rejects tradition
Destructive values	Ill-defined values or none

The Grand Upheaval

I believe we cannot fully assess the effect of our environment on our capacity to exercise resilience without taking into account events that are occurring on a much larger scale at this time in history and that contribute singular instability to the familiar structures around us.

To begin with, we all live with the painful realization of the potential dangers of nuclear war and other threats, such as ecological imbalances, to the survival of life on this planet. The prospect of one's own death has always held mystery and some fear. But that prospect becomes even more terrifying as we struggle to deal in vain with the image of massive death. Life appears to have become unmanageable and unreliable, and the world to have assumed a quality of madness. All too often, as psychiatrist Robert Lifton has pointed out, many of us respond to such stress by extensive psychic numbing, which diminishes our ability to imagine, dream for the future, behave responsibly, and activate our creative powers—in short, our resilience.

Having been influenced by the more optimistic philosophy set forth by the Jesuit paleontologist Teilhard de Chardin, who saw humankind as now entering upon a major thrust in evolution that would be primarily psychosocial rather than physical, I have chosen a somewhat more hopeful scenario for the future. I look on what is happening as a profound structural change in the nature of the human experience and that of many man-made institutions. With the explosion in technologic discoveries, our perception of the world and of ourselves has undergone profound disruption. A television press interview with Britain's Prime Minister can be viewed and reacted to by the inhabitants of a tiny village in India. The enormous ease of modern transportation has produced extensive cross-pollination of cultures and values. The future has moved in on us with incredible speed. The whole earth seems to be in the center of a grand upheaval, which some see as a forerunner of Armageddon, but which I look upon as laying the groundwork for a new synthesis, one better suited to meet the challenges of the future.

These changes are part of a cycle in human affairs that may be easier to envision in a historical context than when one is living through them. Consider that if you are sixty or older, you were born in the nineteen twenties or earlier. When you think back to flappers, bootleg liquor, the Great Depression, and the inaugural address of Franklin D. Roosevelt, the world may not seem to have changed that much. But this subjective perception can be quite misleading, for indeed the world has changed, and one morning you may wake up and find out to your amazement just how much it has changed. Go back to 1870. The difference between the world of that time—with horse-drawn carriages, gas streetlights, royalty on the thrones of most European countries, the United States recovering from the bloody Civil War and the taming of the West—and that of 1930—with telephones, radio broadcasting, automobiles, airplanes, the economic depression, and radical changes in governments everywhere—appears astounding to even the most casual observer. Only writers like Jules Verne and H. G. Wells seem to have anticipated what was to come, and many who read them in their time undoubtedly regarded their stories as pure fantasy. What has happened since will, I believe, be child's play compared with what the future holds.

Most of us, obviously, do not possess much power to directly influence the fate of this larger world. But we must learn to survive within it. Certainly, we can develop the ability to create resilient structures within our own, more modest spheres, and to chart a safe course through the maelstrom for ourselves and for our families.

1 8

Resilience in Family Life

T HE FAMILY is undoubtedly one of the oldest, if not
the oldest, forms of social structure. Furthermore, it has
always possessed an organic life cycle of its own. Two
people marry; they have children. The children grow up and
leave home to begin their own families. Until recently, the original couple grew old together, surrounded by a network of people
referred to as the extended family (although, until the twentieth
century, the average life span was not much more than thirty).

Each stage in this process, from proposal and engagement to
the celebration of the fiftieth wedding anniversary, or to paraphrase T. S. Eliot, "by fiftieth meaning whichever is the last," involves a series of stressful episodes of disruption and reintegration
dictated by the changing nature of the family structure. At each
such bifurcation point, the opportunity for growth is substantial,
but so too is the risk of dissolution. It has always been so, but in
this age of the grand upheaval, the risk has been intensified many
times over. The social, legal, and religious containments that once
prevented the family from coming totally apart at such points have
themselves been greatly weakened, and there is little other than
the commitment of husband and wife to each other and to the

family itself, combined with resilience, to provide continuity. Hence the dramatic increase in the number of marriages that go under.

Now, it is true that certain marriages should never have been entered into in the first place. One or another partner or both may simply have been too immature. The motives for marriage may have been faulty—being based, for example, on illusion, misinformation, or a single dimension, such as sexual passion or proximity, or on the mistaken belief that marriage would be the solution for such problems as insolvency or loneliness. Some marriages are destroyed by psychological disturbances—alcoholism, pathological gambling, child abuse, or infidelity as a substitute for communication.

But innumerable marriages that fail do so for no other reason than that the participants had not mastered the resilience required to cope with the recurrent bifurcation points that arise in the natural cycle of family life. Barbara and Mike Talmadge were a case in point. They'd been married for fourteen years, having met when they were undergraduates at Boston University. On the surface, the first ten years of their life together seemed to go along uneventfully—too much so, in fact. Thus, they never really established the intimacy and communication that could have strengthened their ability to meet future crises successfully. Barbara was pregnant before they married, so their first child was born six months after their wedding. They had two more children in quick succession. Mike worked as a manufacturer's representative for a small company in the copying machine business. In the eleventh year of their marriage, he lost his job; it took him nearly eight months to find another. That was when Barbara started to work part-time. The same year, Mike's father had a stroke and had to be placed in a nursing home.

Unfortunately, Barbara, having been brought up with the philosophy that one should face problems stoically, had little patience with her husband's moodiness and discouragement during that time. He must have believed she no longer loved or respected him, as she complained night after night about his failure to find employment and his sullen silence. He would have had to possess remarkable sensitivity to detect the profound insecurity that lay hidden behind her facade of competence.

With Mike again working as a salesman and Barbara enjoying her own activities once more, this period of stress seemed to have been forgotten. Nothing had been resolved, of course; neither had gained any greater understanding of self or the other. Her respect for him had never been fully restored, and his festering hurt and resentment about her behavior lurked in the back of his mind, surfacing occasionally at night in the few minutes before he fell asleep and being forgotten again when daylight came. When the young woman who worked in his office reached out to him with passion and what he believed to be understanding, he was only too ready and willing to cooperate.

Together, Barbara and Mike missed the meaning of the important disruption that their marriage had undergone, with its potential for making their relationship that much richer. In the wake of this bifurcation point, the marriage remained disabled, finally succumbing to the stress of infidelity.

How might resilience within the framework of their family structure have produced an alternative outcome? To begin with, had they understood how stress works and the very nature of disruption and the need for constructive reintegration, they would have had a very different perspective on the events of their eleventh year of marriage. Barbara would have been able to be more understanding of Mike's bad luck in his career and the pressures he must have been under dealing with his father's illness. They would have talked about it. He would have perceived her empathy and been able to regain his own self-esteem more quickly as a result. And, consequently, he might have grown to love and respect her more deeply and even make allowances for the times when, because of her own anxieties, she could not help being irritable and impatient.

The ingredients that make family life resilient are not unlike those that go into our own personal resilience. The resilient family is elastic, not polarized. It possesses an identity of its own. Its structure permits a shifting within healthy limits, from periods when things are more tightly organized—as when the family faces a crisis together, such as Mike's father's illness—to times when they are more loosely organized—as in the give-and-take among family members when the youngsters begin to show signs of adolescent independence. They share common goals and realistic expectations. A Barbara cannot expect that a Mike will become the president of a large corporation, nor can he resent her for not being a femme fatale in the bedroom, considering all that she brings to the marriage. Empathy and meaningful communications are obvious components of resilience. In a family of two or ten, there are bound to be differences in points of view, sometimes intensely felt; when conflicts result, these must be aired and resolved. The values of the family structure must stand for the continuation of the structure and of resilient features within it; thus, it must often be at odds with confusing and undermining values held by the world around it. Respect for each other on a day-to-day basis may seem like a small thing; but the fact is that in resilient families, kindness, civility, and consideration are important aspects of family strength.

The resilient family is a happy family. "Happy families are all alike," wrote Tolstoy in *Anna Karenina*. "Every unhappy family is unhappy in its own way." The resilient family knows how to engage in creative behavior and to establish an environment in which everyone, regardless of age, communicates effectively with the others. Resilient parents teach their children resilience through the large and small examples of everyday life.

I recall an incident in which one of my children, in her first year of high school, prepared a paper for English analyzing Homer's *Odyssey.* It was a superb essay. When she handed it in, her teacher, before she had even read the paper, asked her for her outline and preparatory notes. Not realizing that these were part of the assignment, my daughter had not brought them that day. She offered to bring them in the next day. The teacher told her that that would be too late and that she would probably take a number of points off her grade because of her failure to pay attention. When my daughter asked the teacher why she wouldn't be graded on the basis of the quality of her composition, the teacher, believing that her authority had been attacked, only repeated her threat to lower the grade. Needless to say, my daughter was quite upset, most of all with herself; an honors student, she saw this incident as a potential threat to her valued academic standing.

Such moments represent unique opportunities for a parent to strengthen the ongoing process of giving one's children a realistic awareness of their own effectiveness, a realistic view of society, and a sense of being in touch with their own emotions and how to direct their expression into appropriate channels. Here is how I handled this particular incident. I listened to her story, told with tears. I calmed her down by reassuring her that I could not conceive of this event affecting her overall outstanding record and by confirming my opinion that her paper, which I had read thoroughly, was excellent. Then I inquired about the notes the teacher had requested, what they were specifically, and whether she been asked to hand them in. Apparently, she had heard and had forgotten. I advised her in the future to do what the teacher requested, since in the classroom, teachers have power, whether it is well used or not. However, I also stressed that there was a point to the exercise and that learning to follow directions was part of her education. I praised her for standing her ground and expressing her honest feelings to the teacher, even at the risk of provoking her. "I think you are in the right," I said, "but you will run into a lot of other people like this in your lifetime. The best policy is to avoid them, but when you can't, then you have to know how to deal with them diplomatically until you can, and do so without giving up your self-respect." What I was trying to accomplish was to respect my child's freedom to learn how to interpret and deal with reality as she saw it from her own, individual viewpoint.

In contemporary America, many parents (and teachers) have found it quite difficult to maintain a flexible balance between being the authority figure on the one hand and the empathetic, listening, tolerant, and perhaps even playful figure on the other.

Such a self-image calls for an attribute closely linked to creativity, cognitive dissonance—the ability to integrate two seemingly contradictory stances, often at practically the same moment in time. The same parent who must punish a twelve-year-old girl for coming home two hours late from a visit to a friend's house must also be able to respect the youngster's right to be angry and must know how to settle the conflict when, for example, her older sister borrows her new blouse without asking. He or she must be flexible enough to change himself from the person who could once order his six-year-old son to take his feet off the dining room table and expect immediate compliance to the person who, as friend, can chat with the same youngster, now nineteen, about his plans for his college major.

Spontaneity is another characteristic of creativity and a building block of the self-reliance that children must gain in order to become effective adults. I am hardly alone in thinking that the hours children spend in front of television sets—however better informed they may become as a result—inhibit spontaneity and foster a dependent, anxious, helpless, and vicarious attitude toward life. Of course, parents can have an even more destructive effect than television in many ways—by ignoring children, by failing to set limits for them, by so frightening them that they forfeit all willingness to risk, or by discouraging them by repeated and intense disapproval.

How often have you heard someone say, or perhaps thought yourself, "I don't want to bring up my children the way I was brought up"? Well, if you feel that way, how can you prevent yourself from repeating your parents' mistakes or, equally problematic, going to the opposite extreme and producing harm in some other way?

Again, the answer lies in your ability to be resilient. Inasmuch as you have undoubtedly adopted some of your parents' parenting attitudes, of which you may or may not be aware, you can free yourself of these only through a process that disrupts your self-image and reintegrates it anew. Let's suppose you grew up in a household where your father worried incessantly about money, although there was enough to pay the bills, and your mother was forever indecisive. If he caught you spending your allowance on bubble gum and other frivolities, you would be severely reprimanded. If you asked your mother to help you decide whether you should wear a particular jacket or skirt to a party, she would never seem to know the answer. Now you have your own children. You've sworn to be neither agitated about money nor caught in a morass of uncertainty. Suddenly you find yourself the parent of spendthrift children who do not seem to know the meaning of money and who turn to you repeatedly to ask your opinion in matters that they should be solving themselves. Your original model of family life has come back to haunt you. What can you do about it?

Apply the rules of creative problem solving to your own behavior. You have already identified the problem as you see it. You might begin by flooding your mind with ideas; you can do this by yourself, with your husband or wife, or as a group, including your children. It may now become obvious to you that in your effort to avoid making them feel less anxious about money, you have always made it available to them whenever they wanted it and more or less for whatever they wanted to buy. To be as unlike your mother as possible, you may have actually intruded in the decision-making process with them over and over again.

To deal with these deficiencies, you brainstorm in search of a plan of action, and finally come upon one. First, you'll put them on a regular, predictable allowance. Second, you'll require them to earn extra money by doing work around the house and perhaps, if they're old enough, taking part-time jobs, as baby-sitters, for example. To improve their self-reliance, you agree upon a rule that they are both free and responsible to make their own choices, except in more serious matters.

By this strategy, you are reducing the hold that your family model has had over you. You are taking steps to rectify the problems that have resulted from your unwitting and unwise parenting. By including everyone in the problem-solving process, you are enlisting collaboration in your effort to change a pattern of behavior—itself a structure—to which everyone has grown accustomed. Finally, you will be examining the effectiveness of your solution in vivo, expecting it to take effect gradually, with ups and downs, over a reasonable period of time, rather than miraculously all at once.

Changing Contours of Family Life

When we examine what has been happening to family life during the past several decades, particularly in America, we might be misled into thinking that the family has become an endangered species. I don't think so at all. Rather, I believe that the basic purposes of marriage, such as companionship, economic and emotional support, and the rearing of children, will ultimately be better served as a result of the harrowing turmoil in which family life temporarily finds itself, part and parcel of the grand upheaval. We will eventually return to greater marital stability and longevity, but by the time that occurs, the expectations of, preparation for, and skills to deal with family life will have changed so as to mature and strengthen its structure. Certainly, the nature of family life has become, for many, a great deal more complex, demanding of its members an ever greater level of resilience, although there are plenty of old-fashioned families around. They consist of a relatively simple structure composed of the original father and mother, children, and grandparents, although the ties to more peripheral family members, such as uncles, aunts, and cousins, are generally weaker. The nucleus of such a structure is shown in the following diagram.

There is, however, a rapidly growing number of families in which the children live with only one parent, who possesses much of the authority and influences the children on a day-to-day basis. That parent is most often the mother. The father is frequently still in the picture, but since the divorce, he has been relegated to a more distant position of involvement. Mother and father are likely to engage each other in frequent conflicts, especially about money. The children may become excessively dependent on the mother, while their relationship with the father

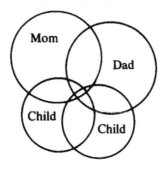

Figure 5.

becomes, at times, quite superficial—he takes them out for dinner and a movie, or on a trip to Disney World. Too often, they regard their father with confusion—love intermingled with a host of negative perceptions that the parents hold about each other. Being a divorced mother or father concerned about the well-being of one's children involves a high level of compassion and managerial expertise. The looser structure of such a family—not infrequently reaching the point of disarray—is illustrated in the following diagram.

We also see the growth of an increasingly complex family structure, one with three or four parents and any number of children, "some his, some hers, some ours." Not only is this structure more involved, but it has been created from the disassembled pieces of former family structures that have collapsed amidst anguish and confusion, leaving in their wake many ghosts and a considerable amount of healing to be carried out. The following diagram illustrates how complex such a family structure is in contrast to that of the simple, old-fashioned one.

It should be obvious that the more loosely organized the family structure is, as in the case of the one-parent family, or the more intricate and complicated its architecture has become, the more the opportunities for incoherence, serious imbalance, disarray, in-

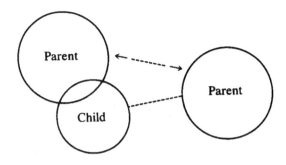

Figure 6.

flexibility, and polarization are multiplied. However, their very complexity can also afford a chance for previously nonresilient structures to become resilient, through the infusion of new and different viewpoints and human interactions.

Anyone who has experienced divorce and remarriage knows how much insight, coordination, patience, fortitude, and generosity of spirit are required to make such complex family structures work. Considerable—at times extraordinary—resilience is called for to weather the episodes of disruption to which they inevitably must be subject at various points and to assure constructive reintegration as the outcome.

Greg Landau, a writer for a local television news show, came to see me a year after he had married for the second time. He was forty-two years old. "I've been under terrible pressure these past few months," he told me. "I think I'm having a nervous breakdown."

Greg believed that his second marriage was in jeopardy. His new wife, Angela, was thirty-three and pregnant. She was also the mother of a five-year-old little girl. "I met Angela two years after my divorce," he said. "We went together for a couple of years be-

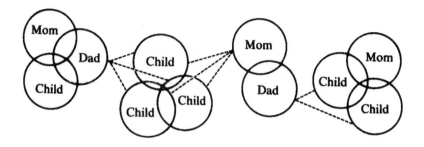

Figure 7.

fore deciding to get married. I thought we'd looked at it from all angles, but we've been fighting with each other terribly, and about everything."

I asked him to be more specific and tell me what he meant by "fighting terribly" and "everything."

"Every few weeks, we get into these knock-down-drag-out verbal fisticuffs. They go on for hours, usually at night. Angela retreats into sleep. I end up staying awake until three or four in the morning. It's either about money, the money I give my former wife in particular, or my attitudes toward my children." Greg had three children by his previous marriage, a boy of twelve and two girls, nine and seven.

I asked him how he and his former wife got on with each other. "It's a strain," he answered. "She doesn't have any real money problems. She married an insurance salesman with plenty of money. They seem to get along. But if I'm a week late with the child support check, I hear about it from one of the kids, usually my son. And we've had arguments about school tuitions. She's living in a nice suburb. I didn't see any reason why she couldn't send the children to the local public school. But she insisted on private schools and wants me to pay the bill." Somehow, the responsibility for school tuitions had not been covered in their divorce agreement and remained open for contention.

"I think she's still trying to get back at me," he said.

I tried to get a picture of Greg's first marriage. He and Ellen had married when they were twenty-four. They came from similar upper-middle-class backgrounds and shared similar values, but their basic interests differed greatly. Greg enjoyed reading, films, the theater, while Ellen was very much involved in her social activities and was an ardent tennis player. From the beginning, each of them took a very individualistic stance, coming together to have children and relate with their in-laws, but never confiding in each other, exchanging ideas, or communicating feelings. Greg had noted the absence of closeness and missed it, but after a few attempts to discuss the matter with Ellen, he gave up trying.

Her affair with an old boyfriend who had divorced his wife shattered the marriage. Seemingly by accident, Greg had discovered a letter from his wife's lover stuffed behind some papers in their desk. When he angrily confronted Ellen with this, she boldly admitted to her involvement and told him that she wanted a divorce. He became so depressed by these events that he consulted a psychiatrist, who helped him through the months of upheaval that followed and in the reconstruction of his life.

"The doctor's moved away, or I would have gone back to him," Greg noted. "Incidentally, Ellen didn't marry the guy," he added. "In the end, they broke up and she married someone else."

I asked him what his marriage to Angela was like, minus their disagreements. It seemed the two of them shared Greg's interests. "There's a different level to the relationship," he said. "We're much closer in many ways. I feel we understand each other—except for the issues that are tearing us apart."

At my request, Greg and Angela came to see me together. I observed that they were holding hands as they entered the room and treated each other with courtesy. As we spoke, they would chat between themselves and with me in a very spontaneous way. They seemed happy and even engaged in a few humorous exchanges. But this mood was quickly dispelled when we arrived at the matters at hand.

"I can't respect a man who lets himself be manipulated," Angela said. "Ellen manipulates Greg. Every time I see that, I get furious . . . with both of them."

"She doesn't 'manipulate' me!" Greg said.

I suggested that for the moment, we table the issue of whether Ellen was or was not manipulative, and asked about the children.

"I've gone out of my way to make them feel at home with us," Angela said. "Fixed turkey dinners on Sundays and urged Greg to take them to shows and museums and other things with me along. I feel I've put myself out . . ."

"You've done that," Greg said. "I appreciate it. But maybe you've done more than you should, all things considered." He was referring to the fact that she held a full-time job and was in her fifth month of pregnancy.

"Money doesn't grow on trees," Angela remarked. "Greg and I have to work hard for it. Naturally I resent . . ." She paused. "I mean I know that he has to give her child support. I know how much it is, and it's not exorbitant. But this school tuition business and orthodontic bills. That's something else."

"They weren't spelled out in the agreement," Greg reminded her.

I recapitulated. "Ellen isn't having any financial difficulties, as you describe it. Of course, it's not her new husband's place to pay your children's expenses, unless he were to agree to take care of extraordinary items."

"She wants Greg to support them in the lifestyle to which she's grown accustomed," Angela interjected.

I asked if it were possible that Ellen might not appreciate the impact that her behavior was having on Greg's new family structure. Greg and Angela both smiled.

"She's really a selfish woman," Greg said.

I noted that selfishness was not necessarily the same as being manipulative. "Have you tried to tell her what the effect on you is?"

"I've never been able to talk with Ellen about anything that matters," Greg said.

"Have you tried, since the divorce?" I asked. He hadn't. "When structures change, people change, just as structures change when people do. She has a new life of her own. Maybe she can have more understanding of how important it is to let you create a new life of your own. Maybe you'll have to spell it out for her. It's occurred to me rather than manipulativeness, you may be dealing with a lack of concern, or insight, or perhaps even stupidity."

"Ellen was never that bright," Greg said.

In my mind I had a picture of Ellen, sitting in the corner of a classroom, wearing a dunce cap. I shared it with Greg and Angela, who laughed.

By changing the way in which Angela viewed Ellen and by encouraging Greg to deal directly with Ellen about the controversial issues, I was offering them a new way to perceive and consequently act to resolve the more obvious sources of tension in their marriage. According to Greg, their arguments about these issues more or less vanished from that point forward, and he kept his promise to try to explore solutions with Ellen. To his surprise, when they were explained to his former wife in terms she could comprehend, she proved to be quite obliging.

1 9

Survival in the Workplace

GREG LANDAU returned to see me again three years later. This time it was the structure of his working environment that had become intensely stressful.

"Eight months ago, I was put in charge of producing the six o'clock news broadcast," Greg told me. "It was a terrific promotion, one I'd wanted for years. Then, three weeks ago, Amalgamated Telecast bought the station. We'd been an independent for years, but old man Harper had to get his affairs in order—he's eighty-four—so he sold a lot of his properties out, including HBC."

I'd read about it in the newspapers.

"You wouldn't believe the tension at the place. Some of the best people have been pink-slipped already. They had new management in place within a week, and the guy running the station won't tell me what they have in mind for me. If they let me go too, I don't know what to do. I'll be forty-six in a few months."

Greg was obviously frightened, although it was hard for him to admit it. The sale of the company had not come entirely as a surprise. He had been anticipating it for months. But during that time, he had felt assured that either he would be kept on or, if not, he could find a comparable position at one of the other stations in town. He'd made a few inquiries elsewhere, and a number of his old friends in the business encouraged him not to be concerned. However, now that the change had become a reality, he had been unable to sleep for several weeks. It was hard to concentrate on his job. Tense and irritable, he was arguing with Angela; her efforts to be supportive were met with accusations by Greg to the effect that she simply did not understand how devastating the situation might be.

"I called my contacts in town. Not one of them returned my call," he said. "Over the past months, they've been telling me not to worry, but now that the chips are down, where are they?"

Greg's dilemma reminded me of a dozen or more executives whom I had worked with over the past ten years, each one caught in the machinery of change resulting from takeovers, mergers, bankruptcies, and other rapidly shifting conditions of business. Many of the very senior executives had been able to depart from their positions with handsome financial compensation, but most of those beneath them were not so lucky. One was an account executive with a large advertising agency who, at fifty-two, had lost his job when the account on which he had been working was shifted elsewhere. He had spent a year pumping gas at his brother-in-law's Mobil station before he had been able to locate another position, with a much smaller agency, at a third of his previous salary. Or again, a professor of surgery at a leading medical school was shaken when his research department was taken over by one of his ambitious colleagues, thanks to a large contribution made by a wealthy friend. Because he had tenure, he could not be dismissed; he was, instead, placed in charge of some unimportant aspect of residency training in which he did not have the slightest interest and assigned an office located in a remote wing of the medical center. After a year and a half of unhappiness and agitation that nearly wrecked his marriage, he finally relocated himself to another institution where, although he did not enjoy his former prestige and influence, he could engage more actively in work with patients and relate; to his new colleagues without embarrassment.

Greg was not fortunate enough to have a specialized degree in a field such as law, medicine, or engineering. While his success had depended in large measure on discipline, persistence, and talent, he was in a line of work replete with competition; younger men and women than he were in serious pursuit of his job, and they were often seen by management, correctly or not, as being more in touch with the times. Moreover, there was a limited number of positions available on a par with the one he now held.

I realized that one of the most serious risks facing Greg was that he might become so affected by his anxiety that his performance at work might suffer at the very moment when he had to do his best. I also recognized that he might alienate the new management should he perceive them as adversaries and assume too defensive a stance.

Confronting him with these dangers—of which he was already aware—I suggested we take a careful look at the issue of compatibility. Did he think he could feel comfortable with the new people who had taken charge, as people? Did he believe he could adapt to their style of operations?

"It's going to be a lot more formal than before," he said. "They're memo people. The old atmosphere was more relaxed. You could walk into the boss's office anytime you wanted and talk with him about anything.

"They're okay, though, and I don't see any problem with that. But I know their approach to the news is going to be different from mine. I've always believed that you have to catch the audience's attention right up front, with local stories, human interest, even crime, much as I hate to say so. They're coming from a different place. They've already made it clear that they want national and international news up front, and I think if we do that, we're going to lose ratings."

The next issue I felt we should explore was change. Greg had already pointed out the narrow range of opportunities for a comparable position locally. He felt that if he sought another job, he might have to search widely throughout the region, perhaps even the country. He could consider going back to writing the news, an option he saw as a defeat. Or he might try to shift into a different but related field, such as teaching in the communications department of a university; but this would also mean less income, and even here he could not be sure he could obtain a job.

"I've been with HBC for twenty years, most of my working life. The idea of changing makes me nervous just by itself. Then there's Angela." Although Angela had assured Greg she did not mind moving elsewhere if necessary, her roots were here, and he knew that it would be a difficult adjustment for her too.

"You're going to have to operate on several different tracks simultaneously," I said. "Thinking of options—in case you get dismissed or choose to leave—and at the same time committing yourself to doing a good job where you are and not letting your insecurity get in the way." Having known Greg well from our previous contact with each other, I was confident that he had both the flexibility and the imagination to do this, even though, in this moment of crisis, he doubted it himself.

He agreed. "Ordinarily, I could do what you're suggesting. But right now, I feel hopeless, as though nothing's going to work out."

"That's another level you'll have to function on, understanding where these feelings come from and keeping them contained," I said.

Greg had learned over his twenty years at HBC to become part of a family. Now, the structure to which he had grown accustomed had collapsed; it was being replaced by a new and different structure, one to which he would have to adjust—if allowed to do so—or which he would have to leave. Leaving could involve geographic relocation, adding another source of stress to the original one. Moreover, his whole family would be involved in this restructuring. Angela would have to find a new way of life, including a new job. They would have to find a new place to live and make new friends. He would also have to restructure the pattern of his involvement with his children by his previous marriage, now ten, twelve, and fifteen.

One of the risks I particularly cautioned Greg about was that of being impulsive. Periods of change like the one he was going through are painful; there is a strong temptation to get everything settled as quickly as possible to reduce uncertainty. I warned him against quitting abruptly, before he had thought his future through more carefully. "It may be hard," I said, "but even if you are fired, try to think things out and not jump at the first opportunity that comes along, unless, of course, you honestly believe it's the right one." For even as the fear of change motivates us to postpone changes that are highly desirable and often long overdue, so, too, the anxiety that accompanies change can propel us into making wrong choices.

My final, and perhaps most important, point with Greg was to encourage him to look at what had been happening as more of an opportunity than a threat. He was in his late forties. Even though he might feel old, he was still young in many ways. "You have time ahead of you to build a new career," I emphasized. "Had this problem come up ten years from now, you and I would be sitting here talking about things from quite a different viewpoint. From what you've told me, you and Angela spend every cent you make just getting by. W. C. Fields once said that 'a happy man is one who makes more than he spends and an unhappy one is someone who spends more than he makes.' Maybe this is the time for the two of you to consider a different lifestyle, somewhere else where you all can enjoy life more fully."

I saw that this option did not immediately appeal to him.

"Or perhaps under this new management, you will find an even greater chance to use your abilities. You'll have to change the way you think about some things . . . news production and organizational structure, for example. But maybe this is just what you need to challenge you."

He had been so worried that until this minute, this alternative had not occurred to him at all.

As the next few months went by, Greg continued to see me weekly and kept as open a mind as he could. He was not asked to leave. To his surprise, he discovered that the station was being run much more professionally than it had been before. Ratings were not hurt by the change in the structure of his programming; in fact, while some long-time viewers might have been lost, a larger number of new ones appeared to have been attracted by it. During his last visit to me, he told me that he was so pleased with the way things were going that he had considered and then rejected an offer of a television job in Los Angeles.

For the vast majority of the world's population, work of any kind is often a matter of life or death, scratching at dry earth in a desperate attempt to grow food, being paid in pennies to slave in front of machines to produce cloth materials that will eventually be shaped into fashionable designs and sold for hundreds of dollars in Paris. I remember seeing a terrifying, awesome documentary on public television a couple of years ago about men in search of gold. I had been idly pushing down the keys of the cable console—a procedure that, understandably, seems to annoy everyone else in the room when I do it—looking for a program, any program, that might be worth viewing. Suddenly, my attention was captured by the deep, resonant voice of a very familiar narrator, Orson Welles, describing desperate men prospecting for gold in the Amazon region of South America, in Brazil, I think. The picture, which still haunts and frightens me, showed tens of thousands of human beings plodding slowly, like so many insects, in a never-ending procession up the side of the mountain in the early sunlight of the tropical morning.

I quickly had an image of tens of thousands of Americans crowding daily into hundreds of buses and automobiles, sitting for hours on thruways, on bridges, in tunnels, on their way to and from work in hundred-story skyscrapers in the financial districts of our cities. It was an equally haunting image, and a puzzling one, considering that here we enjoy the unique luxury of choice. Never in history has a society offered so many people the privilege to choose the work they do, but I am forced to question how well it prepares us to make considered and appropriate choices.

How is a good career choice made? Sometimes by foresight, sometimes by luck, sometimes by our fortunately being guided by accidental circumstances to fulfill our destinies. The best kind of job to be involved in is one that gives us the opportunity to put into play our basic talents. We all have such talents, whether they are as simple as sewing a hem or as complex as higher mathematics or nuclear physics. We can find clues to these by looking back to childhood and adolescence and asking ourselves what sorts of activities we selected spontaneously to immerse ourselves in. Play is an important barometer: Did we, for example, enjoy spending time by ourselves, building model airplanes, collecting stamps, reading? Or did we prefer the company of other children most of the time? Did we do particularly well in composing essays in school, or were we better at biology? Given a choice of summer jobs, did we like to sell merchandise in a department store, work on a construction site, or coach athletics at a camp?

The more the responsibilities of our work afford us an outlet for the talents and interests we manifested then, the more effective and fulfilled we can be in it. When they fail to provide such a fit, many people find a solution in their avocations.

In recent years, I have found that many people of all ages have been having difficulty focusing their energies. Sometimes they have focused adequately, but followed the Pied Piper of contemporary mores down the path to confusion, disillusionment, and disappointment. Many "dropped out" altogether in the sixties and even now constitute the great army of the walking wounded; in the eighties, they have been succumbing to the lure of greed. Today many others, especially the young, seem to have trouble finding themselves and making commitments. Ironically, the brighter and more creative they are, the more of a problem they seem to have. I believe this situation can be explained in several ways.

The first is existential. As we've already pointed out, we live in an age legitimately concerned about the prospects for human survival. The second stems from the fact it's hard to commit yourself to organizations that are as enormous as many of our society's structures have become—large, in many instances, well into the middle age of their own life cycles, and often under the leadership of people who haven't the foggiest notion of how to instill resilience in them. Studies have shown that when any organization becomes too big, it is difficult for most people within it to identify with the whole. Automatically, they see themselves as part of a smaller segment; these segments multiply and become more self-contained as the organization expands. We don't work for ABC Electronics; we work for the southwestern regional marketing division for product X that happens to be a part of ABC Electronics. Even within our own small sector, we may never have an overall vision of what we are about; as a result, it is difficult to derive a sense of identity, purpose, and effectiveness from our job. Moreover, communication within our own segment and between ours and other segments of the organization are rarely catalyzed in a planned way, so that isolation, lack of responsiveness, and provincial thinking set in.

It's also difficult to commit ourselves to something that may well not survive. There has been a shift in our economy from heavy industry to technology, and many basic labor skills have rapidly become obsolete as new time-saving and money-saving devices have been introduced. Economies have become internationalized. Millions of workers have already had to face the need for retraining—a not-so-easy process that involves unlearning and relearning—and have been forced to uproot and relocate themselves and their families in order to survive. Once-rich corporations have gone bankrupt; many small, individualized companies have disappeared through acquisitions by large ones; wealth seems to have found a way to be created, dangerously, without a concomitant increase in productivity.

The odds are stacked against our working within a given structure for the rest of our lives. If we begin working for ABC Electronics in our twenties, the company and its management may not even exist by the time we reach thirty-five. And even if it lasts for a hundred years, our sense of loyalty is not likely to endure (if it was ever there in the first place). Ambition, opportunity, and change itself will probably lure us elsewhere.

What is true of organizations is no less true of whole fields of endeavor. Many young, talented men and women have expressed to me their concern about choosing a career that may become obsolete in the near future. As one woman said: "I know I want to be a scientist. I love biology. But even in college, I was told that I would have to specialize in a very specific aspect of biology in order to move ahead with my career. That scares me. What if I become so specialized that I wake up one morning and discover that all my training and experience has become worthless in the marketplace because of some breakthrough in the field I've selected? My grandfather was a doctor. He specialized in ear, nose, and throat. He practically had to retire after penicillin came along."

The luxury of choice that the present generation enjoys is regarded by some as spoiling in its effect. They consider the way in which young people especially hunt for just the right kind of job only another way to postpone the ending of childhood; they suggest that rather than worrying about what kind of work will make you happy, you should just go to work and let happiness take care of itself. There's some truth in this viewpoint. But, I believe, it overlooks a much deeper current that has been set in motion.

We all have a tendency to assume that tomorrow will be more or less like today. We're willing to admit that change is in the air, but deep down in our hearts we believe that next year, or ten years, or even twenty years from now, we'll be living in a world that pretty closely resembles the one to which we have grown accustomed. Although we are fleetingly comfortable, leading our lives on the basis of such an assumption can be quite risky indeed. I suspect that many intelligent young people today are more than a little cognizant of that risk and behave accordingly, either by becoming more frenetic in their work as a way to deny their inner perceptions of ephemeralism, or by following wandering, apparent pleasure-seeking, nonlaboring, uncommitted patterns of life. Interestingly, I find this trend more common among young men than women. This observation, if valid, may be explainable by the fact that women have in recent years been given the opportunity to carve out their careers in many fields once considered the exclusive domain of men; hence, for the time being, they derive stimulation and motivation from the sheer novelty of it all.

What is quite possible is that today's youth are instinctively getting ready for a radically different future by following a dictum set down by the evolutionists. Overspecialization has been identified as the principal cause of stagnation or extinction in all branches of the animal kingdom, except for man. I never really thought much about the koala bear other than that he is a cute creature who appears in television commercials for the Australian airline Qantas, until I learned from Arthur Koestler that this charming animal specializes in feeding on the leaves of a particular variety of eucalyptus tree and on nothing else. His claws are ideally suited for clinging to the bark of this tree and, again, for nothing else. His lovely face and cuddly appearance speak to his singular vulnerability. Does he have even an inkling of what would happen to him and his species if eucalyptus trees were destroyed by some kind of blight?

To the dilemma of overspecialization there is a possible solution. If evolution is conceived of as an enormous number of blind alleys with occasional paths to progress, like a maze in which almost all turnings are wrong turnings, why couldn't a species retrace its steps along the path that led to the dead end and make a fresh start in a more promising direction? Biology tells us that an evolutionary novelty can appear in the larval or embryonic stage of the ancestral animal, a change that may disappear before the adult stage is reached, but that reappears in the adult descendant. If this tendency toward a prolonged childhood were accompanied by a corresponding squeezing out of the later adult stages of ontogeny, the result would be rejuvenation and the regaining of adaptive plasticity. Such a process would involve a retreat from highly specialized forms of behavior to an earlier, less committed stage, followed by a sudden advance in a new direction.

Perhaps then, in some instances, this hesitancy to commit and the desire to keep options open really reflects an intuitively smart and uniquely creative approach to a most uncertain future and the determination to be ready for it when it comes. To the degree that this is so, preparation for adulthood should bring back an emphasis on a broad, mind-building, and character-shaping form of education, one that requires the study of classics, philosophy, language, history, and ethics, to name a few, as a prerequisite for moving on to more specialized fields of endeavor.

Of course, such issues as keeping a roof over our heads and food on the table don't disappear. What is called for is the creative ability to live on more than one level at a time, finding a place for oneself within the existing system to the degree that this is necessary for day-to-day survival, yet remaining somewhat apart, open to change within ourselves and our world. To accomplish this requires resilience and, as part of resilience, the discovery of a meaning that will give purpose to our lives.

PART V

The Hidden Agenda

2 0

The Search for Meaning

B Y   T H E   T I M E   he was thirty-two, Ralph Bitterman had a net worth of over a million dollars. He'd earned it as a commodities trader. After graduation from business school, he rushed to Wall Street, where he used his gifts to perfection. He was able to think quickly and clearly, and take judicious risks. He had an uncanny sense of when to get out of positions that were about to turn against him and when to ignore the confusing opinions of his fellow brokers so as to make his own independent judgments and hence his fortune. At the peak of his success, he decided he wanted a more predictable, less stressful way of life. So he took his winnings and invested them in a small company that manufactured ball bearings. Unfortunately, he proved to be no master of management skills and was often bored with the business details that confronted him daily. However, Ralph was stubborn and egotistical; he refused to accept failure. In the end, when he was thirty-six, he was forced into bankruptcy by a balance sheet whose liabilities far outnumbered its assets. Not only was he confronted with this crisis, but consistent with his overachieving style, he found himself encountering the bifurcation issues of middle age earlier than most. When he came to see me, he was depressed and had good reason to be so.

I didn't have to explain to him that he had made a serious error of judgment by moving into an enterprise with which he had no familiarity. "I was beguiled by an illusion of security," he said. "With my temperament, I was more secure gambling than trying to become a member of the establishment. . . . But I had fair warning," he went on. "It's not as though I didn't realize I was in over my head. I just couldn't reverse the direction I'd taken. I couldn't bring myself to sell out. Why?"

The explanation for his failure lay in the very forces that had accounted for his earlier success. Being extremely independent, he had listened to no one when he executed his trades in silver, gold, and platinum futures. In his manufacturing business, however, his failure to listen to employees and advisers, including his insightful wife, proved to be a serious handicap. He understood how to take risks that could be undone with a gesture of his hand on the floor of the exchange; in making and marketing ball bearings, he had to plan ahead months, even years, anticipating changes in the industry and knowing that once a direction had been set, it could rarely be changed overnight. He did not know how to delegate responsibility, having always assumed all of it himself. Nor had he stopped to take an apprenticeship in the kind of business he had entered before investing his time, energy, and wealth in it.

"The only asset I'll have left when this is over is the house we live in." Ralph and his wife had purchased a five-bedroom home on ten acres in New York's Westchester County several years before; after the mortgage was paid off, it would probably net them three hundred thousand dollars.

Ralph violated the fundamental rules of creative problem solving. Angry with himself, he persistently obsessed over his misjudgments. He repeatedly compared his status at present with what it had been at the peak of his success. He kept searching for hidden meanings in his failure. "Did I feel guilty and throw it all away?" he asked. (I saw no reason to think this about his behavior.) He had lost all confidence in himself and did not know what to do with his future.

Realizing how intensely concentrated his attention was on himself and his difficulties, most of which we had, by now, explored in some depth, I decided to disrupt his preoccupations with a novel question, one that he could not have anticipated. "Where is your spiritual center in all this?" I asked.

He was predictably surprised.

"I don't have any religion, if that's what you mean."

"Some people find it in religion. Others find it elsewhere."

"Does everyone have a spiritual center?"

"They should. Although I've come to think that if people lead relatively simple lives, they somehow manage to take it for granted. But in more complicated personalities—like yours—it's often a matter of some concern."

He tried to assure me that he had never had any ambition in life other than to make the money that would give him and his family the power and freedom to do whatever they pleased. But this attitude was quickly revealed to be a facade. "When I was in high school," he recalled, "I felt I wanted to do something worthwhile with my life, like most kids that age. College taught me a different lesson. One of my roommates stole five hundred dollars from me once. I went to the dean of students to report it. I was told to forget about it. So I went to the local police. They questioned my roommate, who confessed and offered to pay the money back. The dean called me in and said, in so many words, that if I pressed charges, it wouldn't be viewed favorably. 'After all,' he said, 'your roommate plans to go to law school, and if he had a record, he probably wouldn't be accepted.' It didn't make sense to me, but I knew when I was being threatened, so I didn't. The school wouldn't even move him out. I had to find another place to live. Then there was this Marxist professor teaching economics. When I handed in a paper favoring the free enterprise system, he flunked me. I began to believe the world wasn't worth bothering about."

"Doing what you do well within the framework of a system of values that you respect can constitute a spiritual center," I said. "It sounds as though you never had the chance to formulate this.

If you had, you might not have ended up with such confusion. There would have been a more . . . organic growth to your career. One step would have followed with some logic from the one that went before, instead of taking the abrupt change that yours seems to have done."

He immediately grasped my meaning. "I was good at what I did . . . trading. I do best on my own, guided by what I think, not beholden to others. If that's what you mean by a center, I certainly violated that. And I suppose you could say that I was in it mostly for the money and the excitement, without any larger purpose or meaning."

That was a part of it, I concurred. But I hastened to point out that he had also been permitted to run away from finding such a center by virtue of his sudden and dramatic success. "You were, one might say, carried away with yourself, believing you could do anything you put your hand to. Most people would call the financial position you attained five years ago success. I wouldn't. To me, success implies making it, having part of it—hopefully, not all of it—fall apart, and then finding the resilience and direction to make it again. This is your real chance to succeed."

Ralph sold his home. He and his family rented a much less pretentious one in a New Jersey suburb. He felt he could not go back to his old career as a trader; he'd lost his enthusiasm for it and, he felt, his sense of timing as well. For nearly a year, he worked as a salesman for a business computer software company. Then, with the backing of two old friends, he started a financial newsletter and began a new and what would prove to be very successful career as a lecturer and consultant in money management. "I have the added benefit," he told me, "of knowing that in addition to making good money, I'm doing something important for the people I advise."

One of the most threatening aspects of disruption is the loss of control that accompanies it. Our need to control our lives is a universal, fundamental need. We are creatures of habit and abhor change. Yet our survival on this planet is rooted in the fact we have been able to evolve in a way no other species has. We are creatures of conflict, in search of permanence and predictability, yet immersed in the ordinarily subtle and occasionally extraordinarily dramatic motion that characterizes all living matter.

When stressful conditions confront us in small doses and for short periods of time, when they do not force us to make major changes in how we view ourselves or in the fabric of the structures that surround us, we can usually handle matters with a minimum of strain if we have already made resilience part of our standard operating procedure. However, if a phase of disruption is especially severe, as in a bifurcation point, or stretches out over a long time span—years, perhaps—we can be certain that the meaning we have assigned to our lives is being challenged. We can also be sure that while we may be able to find some consolation in the values upon which we have already come to rely, we shall, if successful, in the end discover new meaning, one that will enrich our life and reshape, replace, or confirm the meaning we had already given to it.

It was Robin Seymour's thirty-ninth birthday. She and her husband, Albert, had planned a special occasion, dinner at the quaint Italian restaurant in town where they had spent their first wedding anniversary and staying overnight at the elegant Brigham Hotel, which they had wanted to do but had not been able to afford as part of their wedding trip.

It was almost seven o'clock. Albert was already an hour late coming home from the office. Robin dialed his number, but there was no answer. No sooner had she hung up the phone than it rang sharply, ominously, she felt, with a premonition.

"Oh, my God!" she exclaimed, biting her lip to the point of bleeding, half listening to the state trooper as he told her, as gently as he could, about the accident. Albert had been pulling over to the right to exit the parkway when a speeding car slammed into his station wagon and it exploded. Two young men, high on cocaine and alcohol, were responsible, she later learned; they were released because an outraged policeman had made a technical mistake in the arrest.

After the funeral, she felt unable to shake loose from her bitterness and despair.

"I feel I've lost all control over every part of my life," she told me, crying. "I can't sort out the pieces. I don't know what to do with tomorrow, much less the rest of my life."

One of our first tasks was to enable her to regain some semblance of command by sharing her grief and focusing on what she could control—the day-to-day responsibilities of dealing with her three young children, concentrating on performing the responsibilities of her part-time job as a production assistant at a direct mail marketing company, arranging for certain improvements in her home, such as a new heating system it needed. But these suggestions did little to resolve her anxious concern over her long-term future and that of her family.

"Does this mean I'll have to live the rest of my life alone?" she asked. "What will I do with myself? How can I get rid of the awful memory of that night? What will become of the children? Should I go on living here, in the house? I'm not sure I can afford to. Or should I move home to Chatham? [a small summer community near Halifax, Nova Scotia, where she had grown up and where her family still resided] How could I ever get married again, I loved Albert so much?"

I told her honestly that I did not have the answers to most of her questions. These, I reassured her, would emerge gradually over time, and it might be better to let them evolve rather than force them into place prematurely. This would mean tolerating uncertainty. I attempted to assess her ability to do just that.

"I was brought up Presbyterian. I haven't gone to church regularly for years, but I still believe in God. I've said my prayers every day, until now. What's happened has made me wonder if God really cares about people, or even if there is a God."

I suggested it might be a good idea for her to return to prayer, if she could bring herself to do so.

"I believe in the power of prayer," I told her. "Whether you call it God or some force in the universe that we can invoke on our behalf, I think prayer makes sense for those for whom it is an option."

She was momentarily surprised to hear such advice coming from a psychiatrist. I assured her I didn't make a practice of arbitrarily recommending prayer to people who did not believe in either prayer or God. But for those who did, I saw it as an important source of strength in times of confusion, a way to find some measure of control over winds of change beyond our ordinary control, and maybe more. "I myself believe that God listens to prayer," I said. "But even if that's not so, prayer reminds us that there can be a personal destiny for every one of us . . . a design for our lives that we may not fully grasp and can't foretell, but that we can live up to and fulfill if we sometimes move with events as they evolve . . . the event, in your case, being Albert's death, the end of your life as you knew it with him, and the beginning of something else."

With my support and, more importantly, that afforded by friends, family, and, especially, her own children, Robin began to restructure her image of herself and the nature of her world. She realized she was still a young and attractive woman and a good mother. She began to regain confidence in her talents and skills.

Assessing her situation carefully, she did decide to move back to Chatham. "It's a small community. I know everyone there. I'll be among friends. My friends here have warned me that if I do that, I'll never meet another man, but I'm not sure that really matters to me. It's what I know as home. If I have to live out the rest of my life alone as the children grow up, I'd rather do it there than here."

Robin returned to Canada. After she had lived in Chatham for a year and a half, I learned she had met and married a fifty-year-old recently widowed banker from Toronto who summered there.

"He has one daughter, seventeen," she wrote me. "She was devastated by her mother's death after a long, arduous bout with cancer. We've become the best of friends. She needed someone like me. My children love her, and she loves them. God knows, I could never have predicted this when I used to come to your office and cry and cry and cry. Is this what you meant by a hidden agenda in our lives?"

The concept that each of us has a personal destiny—some purpose in living uniquely our own, however simple it may be—is an idea that is very much present in the minds of highly creative people. They are in touch with a feeling of being somehow special. Man's religions have also spoken to this point, although many of them have yet to come to terms with the impact of the law of disruption and reintegration on their own continued evolution and life cycle. The search for meaning and the existence of some higher power guiding our lives are issues that many people today prefer to deny or ignore (especially, curiously enough, the presumably well-educated professionals engaged in the work of helping others find their way in life). This is so in spite of what my friend and colleague, Jungian psychologist Robert McCully has said: "Even in the most adamant atheist, religious substance [seems to have been laid down] within the collective layers of the psyche . . . a kind of psychological truth that comes back to us, repeated again and again in different cultures, regardless of their separation in space and time."

From prisoner of war camps to divorce courts, from the hospital bedside of someone you love who is dying to the playing fields where you reach out breathlessly for the will to win, I believe the most vital ingredient of resilience is faith. For some, faith will exist within the framework of formal religion; for others, it lies in the deepest level of our unconscious minds in touch with eternal truths.

If this sounds mystical, it is. For with regard to man's relationship to God and God's to man, all the information is not in. The more we learn about the universe, the more we should stand in awe of its mystery and of some kind of intelligent order hidden within it. At least that's what Einstein thought, and far be it from me to take exception to his genius.

Thorton Wilder captured this spiritual dimension to the human experience in his play *Our Town*.

> We all know that something is eternal. And it ain't houses, and it ain't names, and it ain't earth, and it ain't even the stars. . . . Everybody knows in their bones that something is eternal, and that something has to do with human beings. All the greatest people that ever lived have been telling us that for five thousand years.

Suggested Further Reading

Bronowski, Jacob. "The Creative Process." *Scientific American*, Vol. 199 (1958), pp. 59–65.

Campbell, Joseph. *The Hero with a Thousand Faces*. New York: Pantheon Books, 1949.

Cousins, Norman. *Anatomy of an Illness*. New York: W. W. Norton & Company, 1979.

Erikson, Erik H. *Childhood and Society*. New York: W. W. Norton & Company, 1950.

Flach, Frederic. "Calcium Metabolism in States of Depression." *British Journal of Psychiatry*, Vol. 110, No. 467 (1964), pp. 588–593.

———. "The Phenomenon of Pierre Teilhard de Chardin." *Journal of Religion and Health*, Vol. 4, No. 2 (1965), pp. 174–179.

———. *Putting the Pieces Together Again*. New York: Hatherleigh Press, 1995

———. *A New Marriage, A New Life*. New York: McGraw-Hill, 1978.

———. "Psychobiologic Resilience, Psychotherapy, and the Creative Process." *Comprehensive Psychiatry*, Vol. 21, No. 6 (1980), pp. 510–518.

———. *The Secret Strength of Depression*, 2nd Revised Edition. New York: Hatherleigh Press, 1995.

———. *Directions in Psychiatry Monograph Series. Volume 1: Diagnostics and Psychopathology*. New York: W. W. Norton & Company, 1987.

————, ed. *The Creative Mind*. Buffalo: Bearly Limited, 1988.

Flach, Frederic, and Kaplan, Melvin. "Visual Perceptual Dysfunction in Psychiatric Patients." *Comprehensive Psychiatry,* Vol. 24 (1983), pp. 304–311.

Fromm, Erich. *Man for Himself: An Inquiry into the Psychology of Ethics*. New York, Toronto: Rinehart & Company, 1947.

Ghiselin, Brewster. *The Creative Process*. Berkeley, California: University of California Press, 1952.

Koestler, Arthur. *The Roots of Coincidence*. New York: Random House, 1972.

————. *The Act of Creation*. New York: Macmillan, 1974.

Kubie, Lawrence S. *Neurotic Distortion of the Creative Process*. Lawrence, Kansas: University of Kansas Press, 1958.

Marris, Peter. *Loss and Change*. New York: Pantheon Books, 1974.

May, Rollo. *The Courage to Create*. New York: W. W. Norton & Company, 1975.

Menninger, Karl. *The Vital Balance*. New York: Viking, 1963.

Paykel, E. S., et al. "Life Events and Depression." *Archives of General Psychiatry,* Vol. 21, No. 6 (1969), pp. 753–760.

Piaget, Jean, and Inhelder, B. *The Psychology of the Child*. New York: Basic Books, 1969.

Pickering, Sir George. *Creative Malady*. New York: Oxford University Press, 1974.

Selye, Hans. *The Stress of Life*. New York: McGraw-Hill, 1956.

Stein, Morris I. *Stimulating Creativity. Volume 1: Individual Procedures*. New York: Academic Press, 1974.

Storr, Anthony. *The Dynamics of Creation*. New York: Atheneum, 1972.

Teilhard de Chardin, Pierre. *The Phenomenon of Man*. New York: Harper & Row, 1959.

Index

About the Author

FREDERIC FLACH, M.D., is an internationally recognized psychiatrist and author, who has devoted more than thirty years of practice, scientific research, and teaching in the development of his original perspective of resilience and its role in the management of stress throughout the life cycle. Dr. Flack graduated from St. Peter's College and Cornell University Medical College, where he currently serves as Adjunct Associate professor of Psychiatry, and is Attending Psychiatrist at both the Payne Whitney Clinic of the New York Hospital and St. Vincent's Hospital and Medical Center. In addition to numerous articles in scientific journals and two major textbooks, he is also the author of the bestseller, *The Secret Strength of Depression* (Revised, 1995), *Putting the Pieces Together Again* (1995), and *A New Marriage, A New Life* (1978). He is married and has five children.

STOP WORRYING ABOUT MONEY!
How to Take Control of Your Financial Life

by Mitch "The Money Buddy" Gallon

A simple and easy-to-understand guide for managing your money

EVERYONE worries about money and fear of finances prevents millions of people from addressing their money woes — leading to overwhelming debt and inability to save money. *Stop Worrying About Money!* provides an innovative, step-by-step program designed to take the fear and mystery out of managing your money. It will help you feel more confident about yourself and teach you to handle your personal finances without fear or pain.

Stop Worrying About Money! will show you how to:

- Stop buying on impulse
- Set aside a nest egg for a rainy day or even a sunny day
- Perform plastic surgery on those credit card bills
- Set realistic financial goals...and stick to them
- Reduce stress and feel good about yourself

Mitch "The Money Buddy" Gallon is a professional bookkeeper with over 18 years of experience. Her other accomplishments include registered nursing, nightclub promotion, and house building. She is the creator of the famous Money Buddy Personal Wealth Management System and the founder of the Benebook Library Fund, which distributes books to inner city libraries. A native of Baltimore, a wife and mother, she now resides in Ellicott City Maryland.

PRICE	PAGES	ISBN	CATEGORY
$11.95 Pbk.	168	1-886330-93-X	Personal Finance/Self-help

Available at bookstores everywhere or direct from the publisher at
1-800-906-1234.
Visit our health and self-help website www.takecommand.com

THE SECRET STRENGTH OF DEPRESSION
by Frederic Flach, MD

'Turn depression into expression –
and gain new energy zest, and self-respect..."
– *The Denver Post*

The Secret Strength of Depression, first published in 1974, has been acclaimed as one of the clearest and most helpful books available on the subject of depression.

Now fully revised and updated for the 1990s, this new presentation incorporates the latest discoveries in the treatment of depression, including new approaches to psychotherapy and the myths and miracles of the new antidepressants.

Depression is a normal healthy process, according to Dr. Flach. It stimulates the process of learning and change, and often accompanies major life cycle transitions: graduating from school, getting married, retirement, the loss of a loved one. Depression only becomes an illness when its severity cannot be contained, when a person isn't equipped to handle its pain or its perceived shame, or when it persists for too long a time, often for years after the stressful events that have given rise to it.

Overcoming depression and learning from it is an invaluable source of strength and growth. This positive attitude has made dealing with depression and the process of treatment for it much easier for many thousands of people ... The Secret Strength goes a long way toward destigmatizing depression and encouraging people to take the necessary first steps to recover.

"... There should be a considerable readership for this informed, hopeful, and helpful look at the malaise in layman's terms.. Dr. Flach's credentials lend weight to his views and insights... "

–Publishers Weekly

Dr. Flach is Adjunct Associate Professor of Psychiatry at Cornell University Medical College Attending Psychiatrist at both the New York Hospital-Cornell Medical Center and Saint Vincent's Hospital and Medical Center of New York His central interests have focused on the subjects of depression and stress management for 30 years. His books have included *A New Marriage, A New Life;* and the bestsellers *Resilience* and *Rickie*. He has been a guest an many national television broadcasts, including *Good Morning America, The Today Show,* and *Donohue!*

PRICE	PAGES	ISBN	CATEGORY
$14.95	Paperback 272	1-886330-02-6	Psychology/Health/Self-help

Available at bookstores everywhere or direct from the publisher at
1-800-906-1234.
Visit our health and self-help website www.takecommand.com

CLIMB A FALLEN LADDER

How to Survive (and Thrive!) in a Downsized America
by Rochelle H. Gordon, MD and Catherine E. Harold
Foreword by Ron P. Simmons, co-author of the bestseller
Value-Directed Management

"Can I see you in my office please?"

LATE on a Friday afternoon, those are the last words you want to hear from the Human Resources Manager or your supervisor. That knot in your stomach says you're about to join the millions of your fellow Americans who have been downsized, re-engineered, or restructured after years of loyal employment.

Now there's hope and guidance for the millions of people who have been downsized, the "working worried" still clinging to long-held jobs, their families, and their friends, in *Climb a Fallen Ladder*.

Dr. Rochelle Gordon and Catherine Harold offer inspiring and instructive stories of real people and proven principles for coping and thriving in this new age of anxiety. Although everyone is talking about downsizing, no one is talking to the workers. *Climb a Fallen Ladder* is the first book about downsizing to address employees' emotional and psychological needs. It will help displaced or despairing workers cope with the crisis, maintain dignity and a sense of self at work and at home, and take command of life at the most vulnerable time.

Destined to become a classic, *Climb a Fallen Ladder* is for everyone who works or wants to.

With very special sections on:

• The Working Worried: How To Stay Stable When Your Job Isn't

• Getting Laid Off: What to Expect and How To Thrive!

• Family Matters: In Troubled Times Call On the Troops

Rochelle H. Gordon is the first woman ever to chair the psychiatry department at the John Muir Medical Center in Walnut Creek, California. A native New Yorker, Dr. Gordon has had a private practice in the San Francisco Bay Area for over twenty years. Dr. Gordon specializes in the treatment of professionals and executives coping with corporate reorganization and job anxiety

Catherine E Harold was recently downsized herself from a large healthcare conglomerate. A professional writer and editor for more than 15 years, Ms. Harold has edited more than 30 books and written scores of magazine article on health related topics. She resides in Tucson, Arizona.

PRICE	PAGES	ISBN	CATEGORY
$21.95 hc	250	1–886330–96–4	Business/Self-help

Available at bookstores everywhere or direct from the publisher at
1-800-906-1234.
Visit our health and self-help website www.takecommand.com

PUTTING THE PIECES TOGETHER AGAIN

by Frederic Flach, MD

Every once in a while, readers discover a special book that has tremendous potential to change the way they live their lives. Call it wisdom — or perhaps the knowledge to develop a personal philosophy — presented in a subtle yet powerful way, *Putting the Pieces Together Again* is such a book.

Putting the Pieces Together Again was first published in 1976. The idea that we all have a right, in fact a need, to fall apart sometimes when faced with stress or change strongly captured the minds and hearts of innumerable readers.

Before Dr. Flach wrote this book, the idea that falling apart-being temporarily immobilized by stress, for example-could serve any helpful purpose was alien to our way of thinking. Dr. Flach shows how "falling apart" can often be the only healthy response to stress setting the stage for major advances in psychological growth.

Putting the Pieces Together Again is a stimulating and inspiring look at stress, creativity and change. Today, more than ever, "readers have much to gain from the wisdom and insight offered in this book"

—Library Journal

Dr. Flach is Adjunct Associate Professor of psychiatry at Cornell University Medical College and Attending Psychiatrist at both The New York Hospital-Cornell Medical Center and Saint Vincent's Hospital and Medical Center of New York. His clinical interests have focused on the subjects of depression and stress management for 30 years. His books have included *A New Marriage, A New Life* and the bestsellers *Resilience* and *Rickie*. He has been a guest on many national television broadcasts, including *Good Morning America, The Today Show, Sally Jesse Raphael,* and *Donahue!*

PRICE	PAGES	ISBN	CATEGORY
$8.95 Ppb.	212	1-886330-03-4	Psychology/Self-help

Available at bookstores everywhere or direct from the publisher at 1-800-906-1234.
Visit our health and self-help website www.takecommand.com

WOMEN and ANXIETY

REVISED EDITION

A Step-by-Step Program for Managing Anxiety and Depression

by Helen A. DeRosis, M.D.

Anxiety and Depression are Facts of Life, but You Don't Have to Live with Them!

Single parenthood. Marriage problems. AIDS. Sexual freedom. Divorce. Career demands. The glass ceiling. Run with the Wolves or play by The Rules. Pro-life. Choice. Alternative lifestyles.

NO WONDER women are anxious and depressed. Never before have women been confronted with so many bewildering choices and so many incessant demands. How do women cope? How can they defeat self-defeating attitudes and actions? How can they conquer their fears, win the battle with anxiety and triumph over depression?

Women and Anxiety, first published in 1979, has been hailed as a book that "every woman-married, single, working, or home-oriented-could use to help her live a fuller, free-of-fear life." Now completely revised and updated for the 1990s, *Women and Anxiety* offers readers a new, dynamic, and easy-to-use strategy for dealing with the problems of stress, anxiety, and depression. In an inspiring and practical style, noted psychiatrist Dr. Helen DeRosis will show women of today how to manage anxiety in an easy step-by-step program. With sensible suggestions and solutions, this book will show you how to turn anxiety into a positive force in your life and how to learn to channel it in healthy and constructive ways.

> 'A book every woman-married, single, working, or home-oriented-could use to help her live a fuller, free-of-fear life."
>
> – *Ladies Home Journal*

> "a timely, well-written guide that ought to go a long way in helping today women cope with the stresses of modem life. "
>
> – *San Francisco Sunday Examiner & Chronicle*

Dr. Helen A. DeRosis is a practicing psychiatrist who has devoted years of study and research of the mental health problems of women. Associate Clinical Professor in Psychiatry at New York University School of Medicine, Dr. DeRosis has been a frequent guest on many national television shows, including *Donohue!*, *Good Morning America* and *Today*. A native New Yorker, Dr. DeRosis is also the author of the bestsellers *The Book of Hope* and *Parent Power/Child Power*. She is currently organizing a pilot, grass-roots, family-aid program in the South Bronx, *Parents for the Prevention of Violence*.

PRICE	PAGES	ISBN	CATEGORY
$14.95 Pbk.	272	1–886330–99–9	Women Studies/Self-help

Available at bookstores everywhere or direct from the publisher at 1-800-906-1234.

Visit our health and self-help website www.takecommand.com